AHILYABAI HOLKAR

THE GUARDIAN OF INDIC CIVILIZATION

DEEPALI PATWADKAR

First published by Notion Press December 2024

Margashirsha Shuddha Ekadashi, Geeta Jayanti

Second Print: Jan 2025

Third Print: Mar 2025

Non-Fiction, History, Biography

Photographs: Narendra S P

Design & Layout: Kalaapushpa

Cover Illustration: Kalaapushpa

DEDICATION

Dedicated to the ancient Hindu texts — the Shruti, Smruti, Itihas, and Puranas — the blueprint of RajDharma. While exploring the life and works of Devi Ahilyabai Holkar, I was reminded of their profound impact in nurturing Indian kings and queens, guiding them on their duties and responsibilities, and their emphasis on caring for their subjects as a father would for his children.

These texts serve as timeless guides for governance and administration, while also instructing common people on leading successful yet simple lives. Their role in shaping our understanding of leadership and service is as relevant today as it was in the past.

Devi Ahilyabai's reign exemplifies a ruler's commitment to the prosperity and welfare of the kingdom. As I delve into her rule, I highlight relevant shlokas from these ancient texts—verses that encapsulate the core principles of kingship that were put into practice by Ahilyabai.

ACKNOWLEDGEMENTS

I extend my heartfelt gratitude to Mitra Desai for her invaluable insights that have greatly enriched this work. Her thoughtful feedback has truly enhanced the reading experience of this book.

I am also thankful to Vibhawari Bidve for her constructive suggestions and to Ajinkya Kulkarni for providing essential reference materials that added depth to the content.

My deep appreciation goes to the Social Service Foundation for inspiring me to write about the remarkable works of Ahilyabai Holkar and for generously providing a wealth of resources on her life.

I am profoundly grateful to the past authors who documented the life of the Devi. Their meticulous accounts have been instrumental in shaping my understanding and perspective.

पुण्यश्लोको नलो राजा पुण्यश्लोको जनार्दन:।
पुण्यश्लोको विदेहश्च पुण्यश्लोको युधिष्ठिर:॥

I salute the pious and celebrated kings - Nal, Shrikrishna, Janaka, and Yudhishthira.

Through the ages, Bharat has been graced by many virtuous kings, whose names are worthy of daily remembrance. These kings, celebrated for their noble deeds, were called Punyashloka - so pious that simply uttering their name was believed to bestow *punya*. Among these illustrious figures are the Nishad King Nal Raja, known for his integrity; Raja Janaka of Videha, revered for his wisdom; and Raja Yudhishthira of Indraprastha, famed for his commitment to Dharma.

In more recent times, this esteemed list welcomed a remarkable addition: Devi Ahilyabai Holkar, the ruler of Malwa. Her reign is remembered for her administrative acumen, compassionate justice and service to people.

'*Bai*' is an honorific title for noblewomen borne by queens like Rajmata Jijabai, Peshwain Radhabai, Rani Lakshmibai or Sant Meerabai. Another title '*Devi*' is also bestowed upon noble ladies such as - Gayatri Devi of Jaipur, Sita Devi of Baroda or Tara Devi of Kashmir. The Queen of Malwa was honoured by both titles - Devi Ahilyabai Holkar.

Her devotion to Shiva earned her the title '*Shiva Yogini*'. For her selfless work she was honoured as '*Karma Yogini*'. She was praised as '*Lokmata*', the mother of the people. In correspondence, she was often addressed as '*Shreemant,*' a title for Maratha royal; '*Go-Brahman Pratipalak,*' the protector of all, from cows to Brahmins; and '*Gangajal Nirmal*', the one as pure as the waters of Ganga. For her virtue, she was also called '*Sati.*'* She was a true '*Rajarshi*' who combined spiritual wisdom and regal authority.

Ahilyabai Holkar's (b.1725 – d.1795) rise to power came after the establishment of Hindavi Swaraj in an India that had undergone intense religious persecution under Turkish and Mughal rule. Ahilyabai became the queen of Malwa and took upon herself the task to heal a long suffering civilization.

Ahilyabai's daily reading of Shruti, Smruti, Itihas and Puranas instilled in her values of piety and compassion. It also bestowed on her the knowledge of sacred places, various pilgrimages, and mainly the principles of *Raj-Dharma*.

The lessons from scriptures, along with guidance and training from her father-in-law, Malhar Rao Holkar, shaped her approach to governance, justice, and public welfare. Additionally, from her mother-in-law, Gautamabai, she learned to manage and allocate her private income to the revival of temples.

'Sati' is derived from 'Sat' meaning - truth, goodness and virtue. It was also the name of Shiva's first wife, the daughter of King Daksha - Sati. It was also a title for great women like - Sati Savitri, Sati Anasuya etc. 'Sati' also means a Pativrata or a devoted wife.

In Europe, prevailed the "Doctrine of Divine Right" that granted rulers unchecked rights. While Hindu rulers including Ahilyabai adhered to the Hindu principle of "Raj-Dharma," that emphasized upon the duties and responsibilities of a ruler. This difference in ideologies makes Ahilyabai's rule stand in stark contrast to the British colonial regime that followed. Her focus on fostering indigenous industries, public welfare, finance, and food security can be contrasted with British policies that led to deindustrialization, poverty, exploitation and famines.

Ahilyabai understood that a prosperous kingdom relied on a robust infrastructure. She commissioned the construction of numerous ghats, dharmashala, roads and bridges, particularly along pilgrimage routes, making travel safer and more accessible. Her construction of wells, step-wells, tanks, and lakes addressed the critical need of water in a region prone to droughts.

Devi Ahilyabai's efforts in rebuilding and restoring Hindu temples across India are unmatched in history. A staunch patron of Hinduism, she funded the rebuilding of numerous temples, including the famed Jyotirlinga temples. She ensured the continuity of rituals and traditions, and strengthened the spiritual and cultural bonds within the Hindu community. Additionally, she established Sanskrit teaching Pathashalas, patronized poets, and honored warriors. This significantly contributed to the cultural revival in India.

Celebrated as an embodiment of "Raj-Dharma," she stands as an ideal for leaders to emulate. Her rule exemplifies compassionate governance serving as a model to be followed. Punyashloka Ahilyabai's legacy lives on in the countless temples, ghats, roads, and wells she built, that continue to serve people across India.

In Ahilyabai's life we see this principle come alive —

धर्मो रक्षति रक्षितः

Dharma protects those who protect it.

It is due to Dharma-rakshak or protectors of the Hindu faith and culture, like Ahilyabai, that our civilization survives and protects us.

The book commemorates Ahilyabai's life in six parts —

1. India before Ahilyabai
2. Her early life and influences
3. Her reign, rule of a Rajarshi
4. Her temple reconstruction works
5. Her personal life, one truly fit for a king
6. India after Ahilyabai.

I hope that this retelling of Ahilyabai's works that honors and celebrates a guardian of the past, helps nurture guardians of the future.

- Deepali Patwadkar
Kartik Krishna Ekadashi,
26 Nov 2024

Punyashloka Ahilyabai Holkar statue at Maheshwar

CONTENTS

1. A WOUNDED CIVILIZATION

TIMELINE

Human occupation in the Narmada Valley dates back at least 5,00,000 years, with the 'Narmada Man' being a notable example. Both Paleolithic and Chalcolithic cultures have flourished on her banks.

5th Century BCE onwards:

The Nanda, Maurya, Satvahana, and Gupta dynasties ruled Malwa.

7th – 10th Century:

Malwa came under Samrat Harsha Vardhana's rule. Gurjara-Pratiharas and the Rashtrakutas vied for control over Malwa.

11th Century:

Governors of Rashtrakuta - the Parmars begin their rule in Malwa. The Parmar Raja Bhoja ushers in a golden age.

12th - 17th Centuries:

Invasions bring destruction to Malwa. Akbar annexes Malwa in 1561.

17th Century Maharashtra:

Ch. Shivaji Maharaj establishes Hindavi Swaraj, marking resurgence of Hindu power.

Aurangzeb camps in Deccan and till his death in 1707, wages almost three decade long war against the Marathas.

1724:

Marathas under Bajirao Peshwa with his two commanders – Malhar Rao Holkar and Ranoji Scindia enter Malwa.

The seven sacred rivers and cities, the twelve Jyotirlinga, and the fifty-one Shaktipeeths, along with every river and mountain range, create a landscape adorned with countless shrines. The virtuous souls born here further sanctify the land, making Bharata a Punyabhumi – the Sacred Land.

At the centre of this holy land, where the ancient and the divine intertwine, lies Malwa — a land adorned by celestial, aquatic and terrestrial lines that run across its landscape. The Madhya-Rekha, India's Prime Meridian divides the land in Eastern and Western hemisphere runs through Malwa. The other celestial line - Karka-vrutta (Tropic of Cancer), the aquatic Mother Narmada, and the majestic mountain Vindhya, the terrestrial line — delineate the boundaries between North and South India. Since time immemorial, people of Malwa have revered these lines as living deities.

On the Karka-vrutta, stands the ancient temple of Karkateshwar. At its intersection with Madhya-rekha, in Ujjain resides Mahakaleshwar, the great lord of time. Narmada, flows through the land like a fluid goddess. Pilgrims circumambulate the river and worship her at every Ghat (steps to climb down to the river). Numerous Shiva temples like Omkareshwar and Shoolpaneshwar stand on her banks. Vindhya, the mighty mountain, is adorned with temples dedicated to Shiva and Parvati like – Amareshwar, Vindhyavasini and the mystic Chousath Yogini.

Malwa is a pivotal region where the routes connecting the vast northern plains to the southern plateau converge, making it a coveted prize for rulers throughout history. River Narmada provides access to the western sea, rendering Malwa a strategic place to control the West and to enter south. For the southern rulers, Malwa served as a launch pad from which to conquer the North.

The story of Ahilyabai unfolds here in Malwa, in the heart of India and the centre of the Earth.*

THE DARK NIGHT

In Malwa, where the chants of the Vedas and the melodious singing of Sanskrit verses echoed alongside the chirping of eager students, stood Raja Bhoj's grand Pathashala. This temple of Saraswati, a beacon of knowledge and culture, was about to face the first gust of a storm that would ravage the land for centuries to come.

As the 13th century drew to a close, with the arrival of Kamaal Moulana, a dark shadow fell across Malwa. Like a creeping vine, Kamaal ensnarled the naive, and treacherously converted them to Islam. He fed to Alauddin Khilji all he knew of Malwa.

Information fed by Kamaal became instrumental in unlocking the gates of destruction upon the prosperous kingdom.

Ujjain, located at the intersection of Tropic of Cancer and Indian Prime Meridian is called the 'Navel of the Earth'.

When Khilji's forces descended upon Malwa, it was as if the very sky had fallen. The Bhoja Pathashala, once alive with the pursuit of knowledge, now echoed with the screams. Hundreds of scholars, teachers and students fell, their blood staining the sacred ground. The *vigrahas* revered for generations, lay shattered. Their fragments scattered like dreams of a civilization. [26]

This was just the beginning of a long, dark night.

The 8th century had seen the first cracks appear in the edifice of Indian civilization when Muhammad bin Qasim invaded Sindh. In the 11th century, forces of Mahmud of Ghazni swept through the land like a locust swarm, leaving devastation in its wake. The temple towns of Mathura and Somnath lay plundered and broken.

As if caught in a relentless tide, India faced wave after wave of invasions. Muhammad of Ghuri, Alauddin Khilji, Timur, Babur, Nader Shah, Ahmad Shah Abdali - each name was a fresh wound. First from Gandhar to Sindh, then from Delhi to Bengal, and finally beyond the Vindhyas to the Deccan and South, the invaders marched on, bringing foreign rule and untold misery.

The land that once sang with the wisdom of the ages now wept. Massacres painted the earth red, able bodied men and women sold in slave markets of middle-east, temples crumbled under the weight of foreign hammers and idols that had received centuries of devotion lay desecrated. Great universities were reduced to ashes. And survivors had to pay the Jiziya, a tax levied non-Muslims.

By the 10th century alone, tens of thousands of Hindus were enslaved from the Northwest region of India. The slave markets of the Middle East and Central Asia were so flooded with Indian captives that their prices plummeted to unprecedented lows. The enslaving and slave trade initiated by Arab invaders in the 8th century, persisted under Mughal rule until the 18th century.

No corner of the subcontinent was spared. From the Shiva temples of Gandhar to the Buddhist monasteries of Central Asia, from the Sharada Peeth in Kashmir to the temples of Kanchipuram in Tamil Nadu, from Sun temple of Gujarat to the temples of Dacca and Assam, the destruction spread like a plague. Jain temples, Buddhist monasteries, Sikh Gurudwaras - all fell victim to the unrelenting onslaught.

Malwa's story mirrored this tragedy. The glorious Parmar dynasty, a beacon of Hindu culture, was extinguished in the 1305 attack by Alauddin Khilji. As if passing from one set of chains to another, Malwa fell under the Delhi Sultanate, then the Gujarat Sultanate, and finally the Mughals. Each transition brought fresh horrors.

Across Malwa, temples that had stood for centuries were razed to the ground. In Ujjain, Indore, Dhar, Vidisha, Mandu, and Kalpi, the skyline changed as domes replaced spires. Idols were not just broken their fragments were buried under mosque steps - a constant reminder of defeat. The sorrows of the Hindus - attacked, defeated, enslaved and abused knew no bounds.

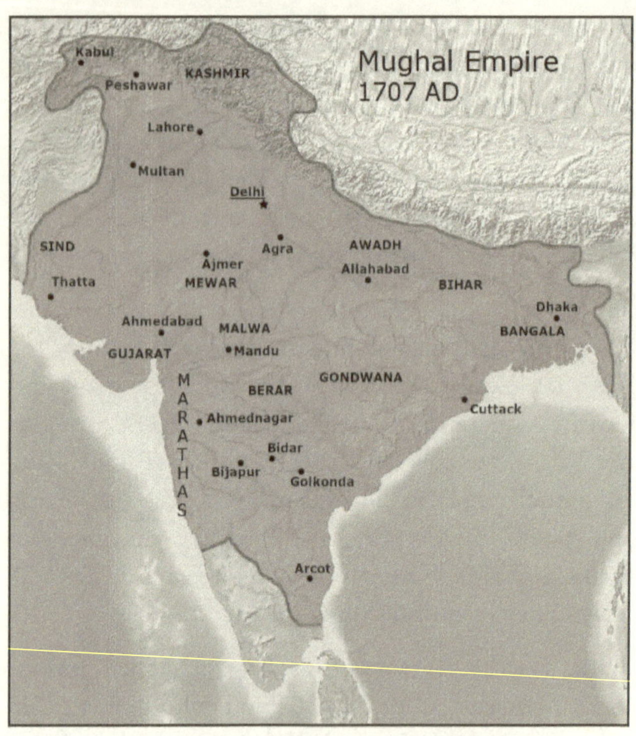

THE EXTENT OF MUGHAL EMPIRE

Yet, even in this darkest of nights, a small flame flickered. From the ashes of the Kakatiya kingdom rose Harihar and Bukka Rai, like phoenixes reborn. Guided by the wisdom of Sage Vidyaranya, they built the Vijayanagar Empire, a grand bastion of Hindu culture in a rapidly changing subcontinent. This kingdom reached great heights of prosperity and stood proudly for over two centuries.

But even this light was destined to be extinguished. In 1565, combined forces of Deccan Sultanates descended upon Vijayanagar like a pack of wolves. The city that had been a jewel of India was plundered, its citizens were massacred and its buildings were consumed by flames.

As the embers of Vijayanagar cooled, it seemed as if all hope was lost. The night that had grown dark seemed unending. Yet, in this moment of deepest despair, a spark was about to be kindled.

Less than a century after the fall of Vijayanagar, a teenage boy walked through its ruins. As he moved among the broken statues and crumbling palaces, something stirred within him. In the ashes of this once-great empire, he saw not destruction, but the seeds of rebirth. This boy became the hope of a civilization that refused to be extinguished. The ruins sparked in his heart a determination that would go on to become a fire called *Hindavi Swarajya*.

THE DAWN OF HOPE

As the darkness of foreign rule seemed to engulf the land, a flame of hope began to flicker in the heart of Maharashtra. Young Shivaji, his eyes wide with wonder, sat at his mother Jijabai's feet, listening to the tales of Ramayana and Mahabharata. Little did anyone know that these stories were seeds being planted in fertile soil, destined to grow into a mighty banyan that would shelter the resurgent Indic civilization.

With the aid of senior administrators such as Dadoji Kondadev, loyal Mavalas and stalwart companions including - Tanaji Malusre, Netaji Palkar, Baji Prabhu Deshpande, Yesaji Kank, Prataprao Gujar, and with the blessings of saints like Ramadas Swami, and Sant Tukaram, Shivaji began to forge his dream into reality. In the mid-17th century, against all odds, the concept of *Hindavi Swaraj* took shape.

Shivaji Maharaj built his kingdom fort by fort. A versatile army became his sword and a formidable navy his shield. Invincible forts dotted the landscape like guards, while efficient administration and fair justice flowed through the land like life-giving rivers. In 1674, on Raigad, Chhatrapati Shivaji's coronation blazed like a beacon, signaling the resurgence of Hindu sovereignty and the beginning of the end of Mughal rule.

Soon, in 1675, Venkoji Bhosale, a half brother of Ch. Shivaji, established Maratha rule in Tanjavur.

After the demise of Ch. Shivaji, the Mughal emperor Aurangzeb, descended upon the Deccan, determined to extinguish this newfound light. Ch. Sambhaji's martyrdom strengthened Maratha resolve against Aurangzeb. Ch. Shivaji's younger son Rajaram, his daughter-in-law Tarabai, and loyal ministers like Ramchandrapant Amatya and Moro-pant Pingle stood firm against the onslaught. For almost three decades, the land echoed with the clash of swords. Aurangzeb lost one-fifth of his army fighting the Marathas. He died in 1707, his dreams of conquering Deccan unfulfilled.

In the wake of Aurangzeb's death, Delhi fell into chaos. Weak Mughal princes ascended a throne that was rapidly losing its luster. As a political ploy, they released Shahu Maharaj, son of Sambhaji, who had been long held in captivity.

Shahu's return sparked a divide in the Maratha throne. It threatened to undo all that had been achieved. Yet, from this turmoil emerged new strength. By 1714, under the astute leadership of Peshwa Balaji Vishwanath, Maratha forces marched on Delhi, their footsteps echoing with the promise of a changing tide.

Around this time, Maratha general Raghuji Bhosale of Nagpur extended the Maratha influence to Chhattisgarh, Orissa and Bengal right up to river Hooghly. To the west, Gaikwads annexed Gujarat from Mughals and brought it under Marathas.

Under the next Peshwa, Bajirao I the Maratha resurgence truly caught fire. At merely twenty years of age, this dynamic leader took the reins of power. Over the next two decades, he transformed the Maratha kingdom into an empire. The Peshwa's sword emerged victorious in each of the 41 battles he led. He expanded the Maratha dominion across the subcontinent.

Nizam fell at Palkhed, Bundelkhand's ruler Chhatrasal was rescued from Mughal clutches, and Gujarat and Rajasthan bowed to Maratha tax demands. Malwa, a jewel in the Mughal crown, fell into Maratha hands. Bajirao's forces marched to the very gates of Delhi, shaking the foundations of Mughal power.

As Peshwa Bajirao's conquests reached their zenith, a new chapter in Malwa's history began to unfold. From the crucible of these victories emerged Maratha Subhedar Malhar Rao Holkar, ready to take his place on the stage of history. Historian Uday Kulkarni rightly terms this era as the "Magnificent Century of the Marathas."

Born in the humble village of Hol, near Jejuri on the banks of the Nira River, Malhar's early life was touched by tragedy. After the loss of his father at a tender age, his mother returned to her maternal home. Under the loving shelter of his maternal uncle Bhojraj Bargal, Malhar grew into a man of substance.

In 1717, destiny smiled upon Malhar Rao as he wed Gautama Bargal, his uncle's daughter. This union bloomed into a partnership that would lay the foundation for an empire. Gautamabai Holkar, with her sharp intellect and political acumen, became his wife, and his trusted advisor. Her counsel shaped the decisions that would alter the course of history.

The couple received blessings of the saints - Shri Brahmendra Swami and Narayan Dikshit, who had great influence on the lives of the contemporary Maratha leaders including – Shahu Maharaj, Peshwa Bajirao, Chimaji Appa, Scindia, Gaikwad and others.

As if guided by an unseen hand, Malhar Rao's rise through the ranks of the Maratha forces was meteoric. A humble soldier under Kadam Bande in 1715, he soon caught the eye of Balaji Peshwa. Then under the legendary Peshwa Bajirao I, Malhar Rao's true potential blossomed. By 1725, he commanded 500 men, and two years later, he was granted the right to maintain troops in Malwa - a decision that would change the face of Northern India.

The acquisition of Indore in 1732, though seemingly insignificant at the time, was a seed that would grow into a mighty tree. As Malhar Rao's influence grew, so did his responsibilities and rewards. The Peshwas, recognizing his loyalty and capability, granted him and his wife Gautamabai increasingly lucrative jagirs.

In Indore, overlooking the Kanh River, Malhar Rao began the construction of a palace. This palace rose as a symbol of resurgent Hindu power, while his policies of protection and privilege for merchants and traders breathed new life into the town. Under his watchful eye, Indore began to flourish.

By 1737 Malhar Rao had become a force to be reckoned with. As Subhedar of thirty Parganas, his annual revenue exceeded Seven Lakh Rupees - a princely sum that spoke volumes of his growing power and influence.

As Malhar Rao Holkar continued to serve four successive Peshwas with unwavering loyalty, he was also laying the groundwork for a cultural and spiritual revival that was to reach its zenith under his daughter-in-law – Ahilyabai Holkar.

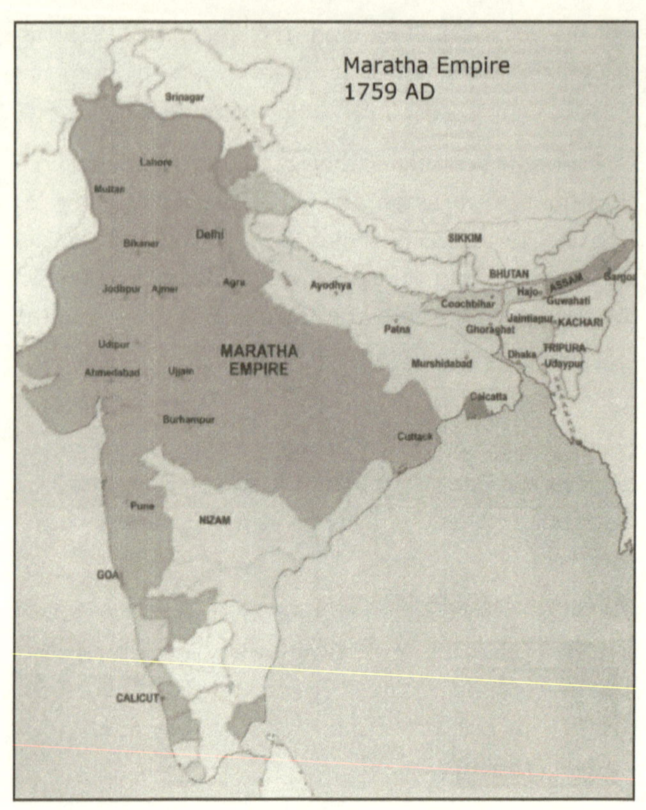

EXTENT OF MARATHA RULE IN 1760

By the early 18th century three major events had occurred – establishment of Hindavi Swaraj, the decline of Mughals and the expansion of Maratha kingdom. This paved the way for the following era of renaissance. It saw the rise of extraordinary individuals who became the guardians of Hindu dharma with Devi Ahilyabai standing as a beacon of this resurgence.

An early contemporary of Ahilyabai was Peshwa Bajirao's son, Nanasaheb Peshwa (b.1720 - d.1761), who played a pivotal role in shaping the Maratha Empire. Under his command, the empire stretched to Peshawar in the north, to Srirangapatna, in the south, and in the east to Medinipur. He subdued three major powers: the Mughals in the north, the Nizam in the south, and the Bengal Sultanate in the east. Additionally, he weakened Afghan control over Punjab and halted their repeated invasions.

In Pune, Nanasaheb developed lakes, dams, canals, water supply systems, bridges, gardens, and new residential sectors. He also built numerous dharma-shalas (a rest house for pilgrims) and temples. His notable achievement was the reconstruction of the Trimbakeshwar Temple in Nasik. The temple had been previously destroyed by Aurangzeb, and Nanasaheb's efforts in rebuilding it highlight his dedication to restoring and preserving Hindu Dharma.

Another early contemporary of Ahilyabai was Sawai Jai Singh II (b.1688 – d.1743) of Amber, renowned for founding city of Jaipur on the lines of Vastu-Shastra and constructing the Jantar-Mantar observatories. Jai

Singh's benevolence stretched beyond the borders of his kingdom as he established dharmashalas from Kabul and Lahore to Ayodhya and Mathura. His crowning achievement was his instrumental role getting successive Mughal emperors to abolish the oppressive Jizya tax levied on Hindus (1713). He further liberated Hindu devotees from the burden of pilgrimage tax levied by Mughals (1730).

Jai Singh II breathed a new life into ancient traditions, by reviving Sanskrit, honoring Sanskrit scholars, and performing grand yajnas. He performed the famed Ashvamedha and Vājapeya yajna, during which large amount charity was given. These rituals echoed the glory of legendary kings like Rama and Yudhishthira; and later by Shunga, Satvahan, Gupta, Chalukya and Chola kings. Jai Singh's reforms also included abolishing the practice of Sati in his kingdom; one century before Raja Ram Mohan Roy.

In Bengal Rani Bhabani (b.1716 – d.1795) held the torch of Hindu renaissance. Born into a Brahmin family and widowed at an early age, she managed a vast estate for over four decades. Her day began at Brahma Muhurta (the hour before sunrise) with prayers and Puranic recitations, followed by the noble act of Anna-daan (food distribution). Her philanthropy was legendary, establishing 83 schools and 33 akharas, building numerous temples, Dharmashalas, roads, and water tanks. The Char Bangla Mandir in Baranagar, the Durga temple in Varanasi and the temple at Bhabanipur Shakti-peeth in Bogra stand as a testament to her devotion and generosity. She also looked after women welfare, especially the widows.

A late contemporary of Ahilyabai was Serfoji II (b.1777 – d.1832), the Maratha ruler of Thanjavur. He enriched the Sarasvati Mahal Library with thousands of books, founded the Navavidhya Kalanidhi Sala, offering education in literature, arts, crafts, sciences, and Vedas. He established the Dhanvantari Mahal, a research institution for producing Ayurvedic medicines for both humans and animals. A patron of arts, Serfoji popularized Thanjavur painting style. His reign saw construction of water tanks, underground drainage systems, a shipyard, and infrastructure development. A philanthropist at heart, he gave donations to support the community. He renovated and reconstructed many old temples, including Brihadeeswara Temple. He also built new temples, Dharmashalas.

A little after Ahilyabai we find Rani Rashmoni Das (b.1793 – d.1861), of the Kaibarta, a Shudra community, who managed her late husband's estate and also expanded it, facing off against the British East India Company. Her compassion transformed the dacoits of Sundarban into a respectable fishing community. The grand Kali temple at Dakshineshwar, where Sri Ramakrishna Paramahamsa served as a priest, remains her most enduring legacy.

These are but some of the remarkable men and women, royals and zamindars of all Varnas, who exemplify the ongoing selfless saga of protecting and preserving Dharma. Their stories, along with those of countless unnamed heroes, illustrate how the Hindu civilization has endured through their efforts. As they safeguarded ancient traditions the torch of Hindu renaissance was passed on to Ahilyabai Holkar ...

2. A QUEEN IN MAKING

TIMELINE

1723: Malhar Rao Holkar and Gautamabai welcome their son, Khanderao Holkar.

1725: Ahilyabai is born in Choundi, to Mankoji and Sushilabai Scindia.

1733: Wedding of Ahilyabai and Khanderao

1734: Gautamabai establishes the Khasgi trust.

1745: Ahilyabai gives birth to her son, Malerao.

1748: Daughter, Muktabai is born to Ahilyabai

1754: Khanderao Holkar is killed in a battle. Malhar Rao stops Ahilyabai from performing Sati.

1758: Maratha forces, under the Peshwas, reach beyond Attock, expanding their influence.

1761: Third Battle of Panipat.

Gautamabai passes away.

Nanasaheb Peshwa passes away.

1766: Malhar Rao Holkar dies

A FATEFUL ENCOUNTER

On a journey from Indore to Pune, Subhedar Malhar Rao Holkar camped at Choundi, a small village nestled at the confluence of the Sina and Harna rivers. Little did he know that this seemingly insignificant stop would alter the course of India's history.

As the sun dipped below the horizon, Malhar Rao's gaze was drawn to a sight that would remain etched in his memory forever. At the village Shivalaya, a young girl stood performing the evening aarti, her small hands moving with a grace and devotion that belied her tender years. The flickering flames illuminated her face that radiated both innocence and confidence.

Transfixed, Malhar Rao watched as the girl completed her ritual with a poise that spoke of a spirit far older than her physical form. In that moment, a thought crystallized in his mind—this extraordinary child would make a perfect match for his only son, Khanderao.

With the decisiveness that had made him a formidable Subhedar, Malhar Rao approached the girl's father, Mankoji Shinde, the village Patil. As they spoke, the threads of fate seemed to weave tighter. Mankoji, like Malhar Rao, hailed from a Dhangar family. Malhari, the Kuladevata of both families seemed to bless this union. It was as if Lord Shiva had orchestrated this meeting.

The girl who had captivated Malhar Rao was Ahilya, one of Mankoji's two daughters among his seven children. From her mother Sushilabai, Ahilya had imbibed practical skills of homemaking, and also profound lessons in spirituality.

Mankoji and Sushilabai joyfully agreed to the proposal. Soon, the air was filled with the sounds of wedding preparations. In Pune, amidst great pomp and ceremony, the 10-year-old Khanderao and 8-year-old Ahilya were joined in matrimony. The wedding was graced by none other than Shrimant Peshwa Bajirao I, whose presence and generous gifts to the bride seemed to foretell the greatness that lay in her future.

As the wedding festivities concluded, young Ahilya transformed into Ahilyabai Holkar, becoming the wife of Khanderao and the daughter-in-law of a powerful Maratha family. With the blessings of her mother-in-law, Gautamabai Holkar, Ahilyabai took her first steps on a journey that would lead her to greatness.

The final leg of Ahilyabai's journey saw her crossing the sacred Narmada Maiyya to enter the land of Malwa. Unbeknownst to all, this young bride was destined to become not just a ruler, but a legend.

Ahilyabai the young Shiva-Yogini arrived in Malwa. This newlywed bride stepped into Indore—the ancient city of Indrapur where, legends whispered, Indra himself had once worshipped Shiva. The Indreshwar Mahadev temple still stands as a silent witness to this mythical past.

In her new family, Ahilyabai found a mentor in her mother-in-law, Gautamabai. She forged unbreakable bonds with Harkubai, her father-in-law's younger wife, and Udabai, her sister-in-law. These lifelong alliances were going weather storms of royal life.

In the early days of their marriage, Ahilyabai and her husband Khanderao embarked on a pilgrimage to Pandharpur, where she adorned Rukmini Devi with gold jewelry—a gift that shines to this day, and a testament to her generosity and devotion.

Ahilyabai's marriage was not destined to be a fairy tale. It was marked with Khanderao's hot-temper, arrogance and addictions. But in spite of it, the brave warrior Khanderao held his wife Ahilyabai in high esteem and heeded her counsel.

In 1745, Ahilyabai was blessed with motherhood, giving birth to a son named Malerao. Three years later, the couple welcomed their daughter, Muktabai.

As Ahilyabai settled in Malwa, she thirsted to know more about her adopted land. Puranik and bards regaled her with tales of Malwa's illustrious past—of Rishi Agasti, who had bridged North and South; of Krishna and Balaram, who had studied at Guru

Sandipani's ashram on the banks of the Kshipra; of valorous kings like Vikramāditya and Raja Bhoja whose legends still echo through the stories of *Vikram - Betal* and *Sinhasan Battisi.*

She learned of the great empires that had coveted Malwa—the Nanda, Maurya, Satvahana, and Gupta dynasties. She heard of Ashoka, who had started his political career as the governor of Ujjain. She heard of the Gupta emperor Chandragupta II, who had defeated the Central Asian – Shaka dynasty to win Malwa. She heard the tales of king Yasodharman who had repelled the Huna invasion. She also heard of Emperor Harsha Vardhana's regime and his vast realm.

As Ahilyabai absorbed these stories, little did she know that her story too would become a chapter in Malwa's grand narrative. Just as Raja Bhoja had once made Malwa a beacon of learning, attracting scholars from across the land, Ahilyabai was destined to usher in a new golden age.

Kavi Kalidas had praised Raja Bhoja as -:
अद्य धारा सदाधारा सदालम्बा सरस्वती ।
पण्डिता मण्डिताः सर्वे भोजराजे भुवि स्थिते॥
"The city of Dhara is protected, the goddess of knowledge Saraswati is acclaimed, and the learned are honored as Bhoja Raja rules Malwa."

Little did anyone suspect that soon, these words would ring true once more, as Devi Ahilyabai Holkar prepared to take her place as a ruler of Malwa.

As the sun of Malhar Rao's victories climbed high up in the sky, a devastating eclipse struck the Holkar household. Khanderao, the brave warrior who had fought alongside his father Malhar Rao and the legendary Baji Rao I, fell in a battle. The death of Khanderao in the siege of Kumbher in March 1754 threatened to unravel all that had been achieved.

The cannonball that struck Khanderao took his life and along with it shattered the dreams of Malhar Rao. The Subhedar, who had weathered so many storms, found himself drowning in a sea of sorrow.

Meanwhile, grief stricken Ahilyabai resolved to follow the practice of saha-gaman*. Had she taken that fateful step and ended her life, the history of India might have unfolded very differently. Malhar Rao, summoning strength from the depths of his own grief, pleaded with Ahilyabai. His words, born of love and foresight, pierced the veil of her sorrow. "You are like a son to me," he implored, "You are my heir apparent."

In that moment of crisis, Ahilyabai made a decision that would alter the course of history. She put duty above personal desires and upheld Raj-Dharma! She chose to become the leader that Malwa and indeed all of India - desperately needed.

---

*Saha-gaman (leaving together) was the distressing practice of embracing death by climbing on the pyre of the dead husband. Incorrectly termed 'Sati' and inaccurately translated as 'widow-burning,' this practice is not even mentioned in the Vedas or Dharmasutras. Though many like Medhatithi raised strong objections to it, it was followed in certain regions and certain clans.

One might wonder, whether the Marathas ready for a female leadership? Would a woman ruler be accepted in a role that is dominated by men worldwide? The specter of Razia Sultan's brief and turbulent reign hung over the proceedings like a tale of caution.

We must know that Ahilyabai was not stepping into uncharted territory. Hindu history is filled with re-markable women rulers. Queens like Rudrama Devi of the Kakatiyas, Rani Abakka of Ullal, Rani Durgavati of Gondwana, Rani Karnavati of Garhwal, and the more recent example of Rani Tarabai among the Marathas - had commanded armies, managed kingdoms, and earned respect and loyalty of subjects.

It was into this long tradition of queens that Ahilyabai was stepping. Not as an anomaly, but as the natural inheritor of a legacy of strong female leadership. Clad in a simple white saree, she took her place in the court, her presence a testament to the enduring strength of Hindu traditions.

The responsibility of governing fell upon Ahilyabai since very early days, when Malhar Rao and Khanderao were frequently engaged in military en-deavors. From around the age of 28, she had begun to correspond independently. She also accompanied Malhar Rao on various campaigns, acquiring knowledge of battle tactics. She received training in horse-riding, swordplay, artillery, administration and accounting.

Ahilyabai would listen to every minute detail that Malhar Rao shared. Like a sponge, she absorbed all that was taught to her. Whatever tasks Subhedar entrusted to her, she executed them with remarkable acumen. Her conduct and diligent work earned her the approval of Subhedar, who, though stern harbored a deep fatherly affection for her.

As Ahilyabai assumed her new role, she continued to learn and grow. The daily readings from the Puranas, conducted by Ambadas Puranik laid the foundations upon which she would build her reign. Ambadas Puranik was a learned Brahmin, who eventually became Ahilyabai's Guru and bestowed upon her the Guru-Mantra. Knowingly or unknowingly, he also played a role of a councilor to her.

The ancient texts, with their wealth of knowledge on history, geography, ethics, and statecraft, became the wellspring from which Ahilyabai drew her wisdom. Indeed her understanding of Dharma, Artha, Kama, and Moksha; her knowledge of sacred places and pilgrimages came from these primary sources of Hindu wisdom.

Yet, the true measure of Ahilyabai's greatness lay not in her learning, but in the application of that knowledge. As she began to govern the affairs of Malwa, it became clear that a ruler of exceptional caliber had emerged.

As the sun of Maratha power reached its zenith, casting its rays from Attock to Cuttack, a storm was brewing on the horizon. The decade of 1750s had seen Malhar Rao Holkar's armies sweep across India, his influence growing with each victory. Tributes from Northern and Central India flowed into Maratha coffers, and the Peshwa showered honors upon the Subhedar who had become the sword arm of the empire.

In 1758, Maratha dream seemed to know no bounds. Raghunathrao along with Malhar Rao captured Lahore and then the fort of Attock, further west of Peshawar. This win stretched the Maratha dominion to the very gates of Kabul. Malhar Rao was now regarded as the most feared Maratha general in the North.

Unfortunately, this victory was going to be short lived. In 1760, the tide turned at Sikandarabad, where Malhar Rao was defeated by Abdali's forces. As if to compound the tragedy, the valiant Dattaji Scindia fell in a following battle. His severed head was an omen of the carnage to come.

Soon, Ahmad Shah Abdali, invited by the treacherous Rohilla Najib Khan, marched on Delhi. In response, to protect the motherland from the foreign attack, the Marathas mustered their strength. Peshwa Sadashiv Rao Bhau, Malhar Rao Holkar, and the Scindias, bolstered by support from Jat Surajmal, prepared to meet the Afghan threat.

Surajmal Jat, Malhar Rao and Sadashiv Rao debated the course of action. Surajmal advised leaving the heavy luggage and the 2,00,000 pilgrims behind the safety of the Chambal. They also discussed the use of traditional Maratha guerrilla tactics. Sadashiv Rao however did not agree pointing to Malhar Rao's own failed guerrilla attempt against Abdali.

On that fateful day, as the armies clashed on the fields of Panipat, the very earth seemed to groan under the weight of the slaughter. When the dust settled, the toll was catastrophic. Thirty thousand Marathas lay dead on the battlefield. Thousands more were massacred during the retreat. The camp followers, innocent men and women were attacked by Abdali's army - 50,000 killed and 22,000 enslaved.

The returning Marathas and their womenfolk, who were starving and beaten, received food and shelter in Bharatpur from Surajmal Jat and his wife.

In its aftermath, Malhar Rao, once the hero of a hundred battles, found himself the target of bitter criticism. His absence during Dattaji's time of need, his earlier leniency towards Najib Khan and Shuja, and his early retreat from Panipat all came under harsh scrutiny. The weight of these accusations proved too much for Gautamabai. Her health failed and she left this world few months following the battle.

As Maharashtra reeled from the blow of Panipat battle, grief claimed another victim. Nanasaheb Peshwa, just 40 years old, succumbed to sorrow, leaving a leadership vacuum at the heart of the Maratha confederacy. The dream of Maratha dominion right up to Kabul and Kandahar lay shattered on the plains of Panipat.

The losses on Abdali's side were no less. He had lost 30,000 of his soldiers and gained no concrete profit. He was also taken aback by the Maratha valor. There were rumors in Kabul of his loss at Panipat. Leaving Delhi in the care of Marathas, he rushed back and never again crossed the Sutlej. Marathas had weakened the Abdalis and in the following decades, Abdali's successors were defeated by the Sikhs, who established a Sikh kingdom right up to Khyber Pass.

Now, even in these darkest hours, the seeds of resurgence were being sown. The new Peshwa - Madhavarao, along with Mahadji Scindia, Malhar Rao Holkar, and commanders like Visaji Krishna and Ganesh Kanade, were going to rebuild the Maratha power in the North. But, that was still a decade away.

THE MARATHA RESURRECTION

As the dust settled on the fields of Panipat, 16-year-old Madhavrao, son of Nanasaheb Peshwa was appointed the new Peshwa. This extraordinary young man bore the great responsibility of resurrecting Maratha power from the abyss of Panipat. He along with Malhar Rao and Mahadji Scindia took up this monumental task. Marathas were gaining back their strength battle after battle. Notable was their victory at Rakshasbhuvan in 1763 against Nizam.

In the latter half of the 18th century, the Marathas had effectively reduced the once-mighty Mughal Empire to an area around Delhi. The two Subhedars - Holkar and Scindia, played a pivotal role in the expansion to the north.

The Saffron Flag of the Marathas was fluttering atop Delhi's Red Fort.

3. AHILYABAI: THE RAJARSHI

1766: Malerao appointed as the Subhedar of Malwa.

1767: Malerao passes away.
Ahilyabai assumes leadership of Malwa.

1767-1795:
Ahilyabai governs Malwa. Her regime is marked by peace, prosperity, and rebuilding.

1771: Marathas capture Delhi.

1772: Peshwa Madhavrao dies.

1773: Peshwa Narayanrao is assassinated.
Nana Fadnavis manages the Peshwa office.

1777: Ahilyabai oversees the construction of Kashi Vishwanath temple, signifying resilience of Hindu faith.

1780s: Ahilyabai deals with Chandrawat revolts.

1782: Construction of Somnath temple begins.

1790: Ahilyabai's grandson, Nathoba, dies.

1791: Death of Yashwantrao and Muktabai.

1794: Mahadji Scindia passes away.

1795: Ahilyabai Holkar leaves the mortal world.

Malhar Rao was constantly involved in battles. In between sieges and battles, at a camp in Alampur, Malhar Rao Holkar breathed his last. Young Malerao, who accompanied Malhar Rao on various military campaigns, was with him at this time. He stood at his grandfather's bedside when he passed away. Malerao, a sensitive youth, was deeply saddened by the loss. The mantle of leadership had now fallen on him and the weight seemed too heavy to bear.

In this moment of crisis, Ahilyabai stepped forward, embodying the spirit of the queen mother Vidula, from the ancient Mahabharata.

यावज्जीवं निराशोऽसि कल्याणाय धुरं वह ॥
माऽऽत्मानमवमन्यस्व मैनमल्पेन बीभरः ।
मनः कृत्वा सुकल्याणं मा भैस्त्वं प्रतिसंहर ॥

The queen mother Vidula had said to her son Sanjay, "Will you let yourself be consumed by sadness forever? Rise! Take actions that benefit you. Do not underestimate your abilities, and do not be content with small successes. Set high goals for yourself. Strengthen your mind and without fear stand firm. Work hard to gain fame and name. You have my blessings." – Mahabharata, Udyog Parva, 133.6

These words, echoing through the centuries, found a new life in Ahilyabai's stern yet loving letter to her sorrowful son: "You must console yourself, for there is no use grieving. Focus your thoughts on governing the state. Let go of any self-doubts and uncertainties. Devote yourself wholeheartedly to your Dharma, which lies in the management of this kingdom. Make ambitious plans, set lofty goals, and pursue those. I am confident they will bring you great fame. Follow in the footsteps of your grandfather and achieve great renown."

Soon, Malerao received the robes of Subhedar from Peshwa. But much to the dismay of Ahilyabai, he was addicted to alcohol and playing dice with his friends. His passion for wild animals would keep him in elephant stables for hours together. As a teenager he used to find amusement in placing scorpions in the gifts meant for guests – all of this painted a troubling picture of a ruler ill-prepared for the burdens of leadership.

The situation reached a tragic climax when, in a fit of anger, Malerao took the life of a weaver. This act, born of impulsiveness proved to be his undoing. Ahilyabai, ever the just ruler, initiated an investigation that revealed the weaver's innocence.

Haunted by visions of the slain weaver, Malerao's psyche began to unravel. The once-vibrant young man withered before Ahilyabai's eyes. Tormented by fears of spectral retribution he lost sleep and refused food. Within months of this incident, barely a year into his reign and at the young age of 21, Malerao left this world, leaving the Holkar kingdom without an heir.

This tragedy, coming so soon after the death of Malhar Rao, threatened to plunge the Holkar realm into chaos. The line of succession, which had seemed secure, was now thrown into question. The kingdom that had until recently, been a pillar of Maratha strength was left without a ruler.

Ahilyabai, who had counseled her son to rise above grief, now faced the ultimate test of her own advice. Could she, who had urged Malerao to embrace his dharma, now step forward to fulfill her own?

As the court held its breath, waiting to see how this blow would be weathered, Ahilyabai's resolve hardened. Lessons she had absorbed from the Puranas, the examples of kings who had prioritized Raj-Dharma over personal happiness and sorrow, and her own innate wisdom all pointed to a single, inescapable truth: it was her duty to take the reins of power.

VICTORY WITHOUT A BATTLE

In the wake of Malerao's untimely demise, vultures of ambition began to circle the Holkar kingdom. The wisdom of Yajnavalkya Smriti echoed through time, offering guidance in this moment of crisis

उपायः साम दानं च भेदो दंड तथैव च |
सांयक् प्रयुक्तः सिद्धयेयुर दण्डस त्वगतिका गतिः ||

Here are four methods of dealing with enemies: negotiation, bribery, sowing dissension, and, as a last resort, punishment or war. A wise ruler was expected to employ these strategies judiciously, based on circumstances at hand. (Such advice is also found in Ramayana, Mahabharata, and Puranas.)

As the dust of mourning settled, Diwan Gangadharpant approached Ahilyabai with a proposal laced with ambition. He suggested she adopt a son, install him as Subhedar, and appoint Gangadharpant to rule as regent. But even as these words left his lips, darker schemes were already in motion. A secret invitation had been dispatched to the ambitious Raghoba, tempting him to take control of Malwa sighting lack of leadership over there. Raghoba, who was unhappy that his nephew Madhavrao had been appointed as Peshwa, was keen to make some gains. He readily agreed and started towards Malwa with his army.

Ahilyabai, her grief still fresh but her mind sharp as ever, saw through the veil of deceit. With the swiftness of a falcon, she sprang into action. She started building alliances, reaching out to Maratha Sardars far and wide, each thread strengthening her position against the gathering storm. She also secured approval from Madhavrao Peshwa for Tukojirao as commander-in-chief and for herself to manage state affairs.

Tukojirao, an adopted son of Malhar Rao, belonged to the Holkar clan and had accompanied Malhar Rao on many expeditions. He was about Ahilyabai's age, but he always respectfully called her 'Matoshri', a mother.

Ahilyabai entrusted Tukojirao with the defense of Malwa. He, along with the Holkar army, set up camp on the banks of the Kshipra River. The other Maratha army led by Raghoba camped on the opposite bank, setting the stage for a confrontation. The air was thick with the scent of impending conflict. It was then that Ahilyabai unveiled her masterstroke. A swift messenger bore her words to Raghoba's camp:

"If you win, you shall earn no fame in defeating a woman; but if you were to lose, you shall become infamous for losing to a woman. Whether I win or lose, I shall earn a name for myself in history. But in your case, know that whatever be the outcome, the result would be disastrous."

These words, sharper than any blade forged in Malwa's fires, struck Raghoba to his very core. In that moment, he saw himself not as a conqueror, but as a man on the edge of a cliff, with honor and disgrace hanging in the balance. The letter dissipated the tension in the air like morning mist. Raghoba quickly changing his stance claimed he had journeyed to Indore merely to offer solace to the grieving Ahilyabai.

Without a single drop of blood staining the sacred waters of the Kshipra, Ahilyabai had emerged triumphant. In a final act of magnanimity, Ahilyabai extended an invitation to Raghoba, welcoming him to Indore not as a vanquished foe, but as an honored guest. As they shared their meals in the Holkar palace, the echoes of the impending disaster faded away and were replaced by the promise of a peaceful future.

This bloodless victory stood as a testament to Ahilyabai's mastery of statecraft. She had employed the first three methods outlined in the ancient texts - negotiation (in inviting Raghoba as a guest), bribery (in the form of political alliances), and sowing dissension (through her clever message) - avoiding the need for the fourth and most costly option of war.

In this moment of triumph, Ahilyabai had secured her position while demonstrating a level of wisdom and foresight that would become the hallmark of her reign. She was the queen who could win battles without drawing a sword. The reign of Ahilyabai Holkar had truly begun…

Ahilyabai moved swiftly to consolidate her power. Taking charge of the state, she stationed Tukojirao, her trusted general, at Indore as the commander-in-chief, while she retreated to her new residence on the tranquil banks of the Narmada at Maheshwar. She oversaw state affairs and Khasgi from there.

This arrangement, born of mutual trust and respect, was destined to endure throughout Ahilyabai's lifetime. Yet, as the years passed, the seeds of discord began to take root. Tukojirao started to overstep his bounds and made decisions without consultation. It was a clear affront to Ahilyabai's authority.

The issue of finances became a particular point of contention. Tradition dictated that tributes collected during military campaigns be divided meticulously - a portion for the Peshwas as taxes, another for military expenses, and the remainder added to state coffers. Tukojirao, however, instead of adding to the Daulat, spent funds from the state treasury. Each demand chipped away at the fragile peace between queen and commander.

As tensions simmered, Tukojirao sought help from outside, Mahadji Scindia. He approached Ahilyabai and condescendingly suggested that he and Tukojirao could take control of everything she owned. In response Ahilyabai warned Mahadji, in no uncertain terms, that any attempt to usurp her power would result in their arrest. The image she conjured - of would-be usurpers chained to the legs of elephants and dragged through the streets - was as vivid as it was terrifying.

Mahadji, wisely recognizing the folly of his words, retreated, never again daring to interfere in Ahilyabai's affairs. Yet the issue with Tukojirao persisted, a thorn in the side of her reign that even Nana Fadnavis would not try to remove.

Despite such challenges, Ahilyabai's grip on power never wavered. Though Tukojirao held the title of Subhedar, it was Ahilyabai who truly ruled. Her authority, earned through wisdom, courage, commitment to her people, and her loyalty to the Peshwas was absolute.

This period of Ahilyabai's reign serves as a masterclass in statecraft. She demonstrated the ability to delegate authority without relinquishing control, to trust without being naive, and to wield power without resorting to unnecessary brutality. Her warning to Mahadji, while fierce, was ultimately bloodless - another example of her preference for wisdom over violence.

Ahilyabai, who could win battles with words and secure her throne with a single, well-placed threat, was proving to be a ruler of exceptional caliber. She could stand firm against internal and external threats and establish her control, firmly and fairly.

The iron hand in the velvet glove - this was Ahilyabai Holkar. A queen who was as gentle as the flowing Narmada, as unyielding as the mighty Vindhyas, and as bounded by Raj-Dharma as the Sun is by the Karka-Vrutta.

As Ahilyabai Holkar ascended to power, the simmering discontent in Rampur erupted into Chandrawat revolts. Rampur was populated by an Udaipur prince with aid of Chandrawats who later settled there. They harbored resentment since Madho Singh, son of Raja Jai Singh of Jaipur, ceded Rampur to Subhedar Malhar Rao in 1759. Dissatisfaction brewed, but as long as Malhar Rao was around, they stayed quiet. After his demise, the unrest surfaced.

In 1768, Ahilyabai extended an olive branch, granting the Chandrawats 31 villages in a bid for reconciliation. This gesture of goodwill bought a brief respite, but peace proved fragile. In 1771, seizing the chance of Tukojirao's absence, the Chandrawats struck. Despite her depleted forces, Ahilyabai's army, led by Shariff Bhai, emerged victorious. True to her nature, she sealed the victory not with punishment, but with a treaty.

Yet the embers of revolt continued to smolder. Another uprising was quelled by Devi's forces under Laxman Tandeo, again followed by a treaty and a generous grant of 7,000 rupees. In 1787, Chandrawats allied with Rajputs and mounted their most formidable challenge. In this fierce battle, Devi's army was commanded by Abajipant and Ragho Ranchhod. She also sought Scindia's assistance and sent an additional unit led by her brother, Tulaji Shinde. This time a complete victory was achieved, some rebel leaders were given capital punishment, some were imprisoned, tributes were collected and surety of good behavior was secured.

This series of conflicts, the only major battles in her 27-year reign, showcased Ahilyabai's multifaceted approach to leadership. Her primary policy was peace, pursued through diplomacy and reconciliation. Yet when necessary, she did not hesitate to wield the sword. Most remarkably, her victories were always followed by merciful treaties, a testament to her commitment to long-term stability over short-term retribution.

RULE OF RIGHTEOUSNESS

Ahilyabai's approach to governance was deeply rooted in the ancient concept of Raj-Dharma, the righteous duties and responsibilities of a ruler. This philosophy, expounded in texts like the Ramayana, Mahabharata, and Puranas, provided a comprehensive framework for just and effective rule.

Daily, Ahilyabai immersed herself in these texts, absorbing their wisdom and applying it to her reign. Her understanding of Raj-Dharma is encapsulated in her statement: "Sarkar is not mere government. It is the people's maay-baap (mother and father)."

Ahilyabai's approach to governance is a sentiment echoed that is echoed in this teaching from the Arthashastra:

प्रजा-सुखे सुखं राज्ञः प्रजानां च हिते हितं ।

नऽत्म-प्रियं हितं राज्ञः प्रजानां तु प्रियं हितं ॥

A king's well-being and happiness lies in the happiness and well-being of his subjects. A king's happiness lies not in his own well-being, or in his own likes and dislikes.

Ahilyabai saw her role not as a privilege, but as a sacred duty bestowed by Shiva himself. Her words, "I possess no wealth; I merely facilitate its return to its rightful owner," reflect a profound understanding of kingship as stewardship rather than ownership.

The Indian philosophy of Raj-Dharma stood in stark contrast to the European "Doctrine of Divine Right," which granted monarchs absolute authority and no accountability. The Divine Rights were used to justify their power and legitimacy for centuries. (As a reaction to Divine Rights, the concept of Human Rights was born and became significant after World War II in 1948.)

In Europe, tales of benevolent kings were rare even in the folk lore. In absence of a guide, and a model for kings to follow, rulers who truly nurtured and protected their subjects were rare and if so, self-made. Most western monarchs focused on building lavish palaces, accumulating vast riches and indulging in extravagance. Many resorted to persecuting dissenters, oppressing their own subjects, and attacking neighbors for religious expansion.

European folklore often portrayed rulers as distant and unjust, necessitating figures like Robin Hood to redistribute wealth, Ahilyabai's reign embodied the ideal of a ruler who was herself the benefactor of her people. Her approach left British administrators like Sir John Malcolm and poetess Joanne Baillie in awe. They witnessed a ruler who, guided by ancient wisdom, had created a system of governance that prioritized the welfare of her subjects, from the highest noble to the lowliest peasant.

In Ahilyabai Holkar, the concept of Raj-Dharma found its living embodiment. Her reign was a testament to the enduring power of righteous rule.

As Ahilyabai navigated the challenges of governance, from quelling revolts to managing daily affairs, she demonstrated that wisdom, compassion, and justice were not lofty ideals, but practical principles.

Ahilyabai's attitude towards her duty reflects what king Rantidev asked for as a boon in Bhāgvat Purana-

"न त्वहं कामये राज्यं न स्वर्गं नापुनर्भवम् ।

कामये दुःखतप्तानां प्राणिनामार्तिनाशनम् ॥"

King Rantidev had said, "Oh Vishnu! I seek not kingdom while I live, nor do I seek the heavens after I die. All that I wish for is to end the sufferings of all my subjects — men, women, animals, and all the living beings in my kingdom."

HOLISTIC ADMINISTRATION

In the annals of Indian statecraft, the wisdom of Chanakya's Arthashastra has long been revered. The seven limbs of administration mentioned by him were reiterated by later authors such as - Ramchandrapant Amatya in the *Adnyapatre.**

**Ramchandrapant a minister of Ch. Shivaji and a disciple of Ramadas Swami, was a statesman and a warrior. In his later years he wrote Adnyapatra, in which he described the principles of state policy about the rule of Chhatrapati; written as if those were his orders on how to govern.*

The seven limbs of administration are - Swami, Amatya, Rashtra, Durga, Kosha, Danda, and Mitra - form the backbone of effective governance. Ahilyabai Holkar, in her reign, understood these principles and breathed life into them. V. V. Thakur analyzes Ahilyabai's rule at length based on these seven principles in the book "Life and life's work of Shri Devi Ahilya Bai Holkar" -

1. Swami (Monarch):

Though Tukojirao held the title of Subhedar, it was Ahilyabai who truly ruled. Her daily routine mirrored that of a diligent king. With an encyclopedic knowledge of her territory and a keen understanding of both foreign and domestic policy, she navigated the complex political landscape with grace.

Ahilyabai's loyalty to the Peshwas, coupled with a sense of unity amongst the Marathas showcased her strategic thinking. At home, she struck a delicate balance - treating subordinates with respect while maintaining strict oversight of their work.

2. Amatya (Ministers):

Ahilyabai's court was a blend of experience and fresh perspectives. Ministers like Chandrachud and Palsikar, holdovers from Malhar Rao's time, provided continuity, while new appointees like Mukundarao and Govindpant Ganu brought fresh ideas.

Her practice of listening to all counsel before making her decisions ensured a well-rounded approach to governance. This collaborative yet decisive leadership style was the key to her successful regime.

3. Rashtra (People):

The welfare of her subjects was always at the fore-front. Ahilyabai provided for food, clothing, water and livelihood to the people in Malwa and beyond. Remarkably, while famines ravaged other parts of Central India, Malwa remained untouched during her reign. Her accessibility to her subjects, allowing them to approach her directly for help or justice, fostered a deep connection between the rulers and ruled.

4. Durga (Forts):

Though the strategic importance of forts had diminished by Ahilyabai's time, she maintained them diligently. The forts at Maheshwar, Chandwad, Asirgarh, and others were symbols of Holkar power. In 1767 she made Maheshwar Fort her residence breathing new life into it.

5. Kosha (Treasury):

Ahilyabai's policies encouraged business and industry, made travel safe for merchants, provided low-interest loans for new businesses, and improved agricultural infrastructure. These measures improved the lives of her subjects and also filled the state coffers.

6. Danda (Army / Justice / Law & Order):

Ahilyabai maintained a well-equipped army, complete with elephants, horses, and the latest in artillery. Under Malhar Rao, she had in Gwalior established an artillery factory. Recognizing the growing threat from the British, she later employed European trainers for her army. She used military force judiciously, preferring diplomacy but not hesitating to take up arms when necessary.

7. Mitra (Allies):

Ahilyabai maintained a network of ambassadors across Indian states, from Hyderabad to Lucknow and Delhi to Pune. Her ability to resolve disputes in other states spoke of her reputation as a fair and wise ruler. She had the foresight to recognize the threat posed by British. Her call for Indian states to unite against this common foe was visionary.

Ahilyabai Holkar's reign was a living embodiment of the seven principles of administration. Her holistic approach to governance - balancing military might with diplomatic finesse, economic prosperity with social welfare, and personal leadership with collaborative decision-making - created a golden age in Malwa's history.

AHILYABAI'S GOVERNANCE

"तेन धर्मोत्तरश्चायं कृतो लोको महात्मना
रञ्जिताश्च प्रजाः सर्वास्तेन राजेति शब्द्यते"

That great soul instilled righteousness throughout the world. Because he brought joy to his subjects, he earned the title of 'Raja'. Mahabharata, Shanti Parva 58.133

This ancient wisdom from the Mahabharata was exemplified in Ahilyabai Holkar's reign. Her governance was not merely about maintaining law and order; it was a rule for the people.

In a stark departure from the Mughals who imposed Farsi, Ahilyabai embraced the language of her people. Though a Marathi speaker herself, she did not force her native tongue on the Hindi/Khadi Boli speakers of Malwa. This subject-friendly aspect was seen in every facet of Ahilyabai's governance.

Every directive of Ahilyabai was issued "By the order of Shiva" (Shree Shankar Adnyevarun), and even her coins bore the imprint of the Shivalinga and Bel Patra. It reflected her deep-seated belief in ruling as a form of seva and devotion.

FINANCIAL ACUMEN

Ahilyabai's mastery of finance is not a well known aspect. She was a queen who understood the Mahabharata's teaching that wealth is the foundation of all virtues:

"धर्मः कामश्च स्वर्गश्च हर्षः क्रोधः श्रुतं दमः

अर्थादितानि सर्वाणि प्रवर्तन्ते नराधिप"

Dharma (fulfilling duties and responsibilities), Kama (enjoying pleasures), Swarga (heaven after death), joy, anger, knowledge, and control over the senses all are attainable only through Artha (wealth). Just as rivers originate from mountains, Dharma originates from Artha.

- *Mahabharata, Shanti Parva, 8.22-23*

Her strict financial management extended even to her family. She didn't hesitate to reprimand her husband Khanderao for overspending or to classify her father-in-law's religious expenditures as personal costs.

Whether it was her philanthropy, or her welfare works, or her compassionate policy towards Bhil community, or her agricultural initiatives all of it led to improved economy.

Ahilyabai's financial policies and charities extended beyond personal philanthropy. By providing low-interest loans to businessmen, she stimulated economic growth, increasing state revenue from 65 Lakh to 1.5 Crore. Her reforms in land ownership and taxation further bolstered the economy.

CHARITABLE INITIATIVES

The concept of Stree-Dhan (women's wealth) found a grand expression in Ahilyabai's reign. The Khasgi trust, initially set up for Gautamabai, became a powerful tool in the hands of Ahilyabai. Gautamabai left in the account 16 crore rupees. With this wealth at disposal, Ahilyabai chose to invest it in temples and public works rather than personal luxuries.

In regard of putting Stree-dhan to right use, Gautamabai and later Ahilyabai followed in the footsteps of Kausalya Devi, the revered mother of Rama. Ramayana mentions -

कौसल्या बिभृयात् आर्या सहस्रम् अपि मद् विधान् |
यस्याः सहस्रम् ग्रामाणाम् सम्प्राप्तम् उपजीवनम् || २-३१-२०

Kausalya was entrusted with the income of a thousand villages. She utilized it for the welfare of a thousand people who sought shelter and depended on her.

Like Kausalya, Gautamabai and Ahilyabai dedicated their personal resources to the welfare of the people, embodying the same spirit of service and generosity.

Through strict checks, Ahilyadevi ensured that her charity went to those who deserved. Her donations were *sat-patri-daan* (given to those who would put it to good use.) Her appointment of Govindpant Ganu to manage the Khasgi showcased her talent for selecting the right person for the right job. Under him the funds were used judiciously for charitable institutions and endowments.

EDUCATIONAL INITIATIVES

Ahilyabai understood the profound truth expressed in the Bhāgvat Purana:

"य उद्धरेत्करं राजा प्रजा धर्मेष्वशिक्षयन्।

प्रजानां शमलं भुङ्क्ते भगं च स्वं जहाति सः"

A king who only collects taxes without imparting moral education shares in his subjects' sins and loses his glory. - Bhāgvat Purana (1.21.24)

Ahilyabai promoted literacy, established Sanskrit schools, and encouraged the study of ancient texts. She founded a colony named Brahmapuri in Benares for Sanskrit teaching. It was a settlement of learned Bramhins, who would dedicate their lives to learning and teaching Sanskrit. This was a visionary step towards preserving and propagating learning.

She invited learned pundits and physicians to Maheshwar. She honoured learned people, and whenever such people wished to travel north to Benares, the city of learning, she made sufficient provisions for their travel.

Ahilyabai's personal dedication to learning - her book collection, her daily study of Puranas, her patronage for scholars, her organization of communal reading of Puranas - set an example that rippled through her court. Ahilya Devi's actions were imitated by her courtiers. They too entertained scholars at their residences, arranged Purana retelling, and gave donations for such activities.

AHILYABAI'S JUDICIARY

Ahilyabai Holkar's reign stands for its exemplary system of justice. Her deep understanding of human nature, coupled with an unwavering commitment to justice and her people, made her court a beacon of hope for the aggrieved and oppressed.

Ahilyabai's reputation as a just and impartial judge drew people from all walks of life to seek her counsel. Her judgments, delivered with precision, left even the most contentious parties satisfied. Cases that came to her were diverse, ranging from land disputes and matters of adoption to financial matters and murders, each was handled with equal care and consideration.

In one notable case, she meticulously examined ownership documents to restore land to its rightful owner, Maniram Choudhary, from an encroaching landlord. In another instance, she demonstrated her commitment to financial integrity by ensuring that villagers who had lent money to a traveler were reimbursed, while also establishing a system to recover the debt from the borrower.

Ahilyabai's court was particularly noteworthy for its accessibility to women. Her empathy for their plight and her staunch defense of women's dignity set a new standard for gender equality in judicial matters.

Two cases in particular, involving widows seeking to adopt a child highlight her compassionate approach. In both instances, Ahilyabai waived hefty fees and fines, allowing the women to fulfill their wishes without financial burden.

It is said that Ahilyabai employed the widows of soldiers in the textile industry, thus offering them dignified livelihoods.

Once, Raghoba along with his army went by the way of Maheshwar to the north on some expedition. On his way he took 8 bullocks from Kirsana village. Ahilyabai compensated the village for the loss.

Devi's reputation for delivering fair justice reached far beyond Malwa. Royals from other princely states sought her counsel to resolve their internal disputes, a testament to her wisdom and impartiality.

Ahilyabai treated her people with the same care and concern as she would treat her own children. Her administration remained vigilant ensuring that justice was accessible and impartial to all.

HANDLING THUGEES

The reign of Ahilyabai Holkar was marked by her innovative and humane approach to governance, particularly evident in her handling of the Bhil, Gond, and

Ramoshi communities. These groups, notorious for their criminal activities in the Nimar and Khandesh regions, posed a significant challenge to law and order.

Initially, the Peshwas had attempted to control them through harsh measures, including capital punishment. However, this approach proved ineffective. When Ahilyabai assumed control, she first tried military operations led by Yashwantrao Phanse and Satwaji Paykawad, but soon realized the futility of this strategy.

Ahilyabai, it seems, understood the profound truth expressed in the Bhāgvat Purana:

"यस्य राष्ट्रे प्रजाः सर्वास्त्रस्यन्ते साध्व्यसाधुभिः।

तस्य मत्तस्य नश्यन्ति कीर्तिरायुर्भगो गतिः"

If a kingdom is plagued by the misdeeds of the wicked, its king loses his reputation, longevity, wealth, and the promise of Swarga after death.

To solve the problem of the criminal activities, in a remarkable shift, Ahilyabai adopted a compassionate approach. She offered them better livelihood options including agricultural and occupational opportunities. She acknowledged their land rights, and allowed them to collect taxes on the goods thoroughfare. Through these measures she effectively prevented their need to adopt criminal activities.

With these changes, Ahilyabai held the Bhil community responsible for any looting in their area. Actively monitoring their activities, if any trader was looted on his way, she made the responsible Bhill compensate the trader for his loss. She thus transformed them from potential criminals into protectors of lone travelers and merchant caravans.

This approach improved the lives of these communities and also led to the flourishing of business and prosperity in her realm. Such was the impact of her benevolent actions that she came to be regarded as a "Devi" by these very people.

The wisdom and compassion in Ahilyabai's approach becomes even more apparent when contrasted with the later British handling of similar issues. The British Thuggee Act of 1836 and the subsequent Criminal Tribes Act of 1871 criminalized entire communities, leading to severe human rights abuses. Anyone born in these communities was presumed to be a "born criminal". Generations of these communities suffered due to the inhuman British policy. By 1947, over 13 million people of 127 different communities were subject to arbitrary search and arrest. The act was repealed soon after independence, in August 1949.

The European treatment of India's nomadic tribes was a continuation of how the Roma, the nomadic tribes of Europe were treated. By World War II, the hatred against the nomadic tribes led to their ethnic cleansing, widespread persecution, and genocide in the Nazi concentration camps. By the end of WWII, it is estimated that about 25% of the Roma population had perished. Indian nomadic tribes faced similar prejudice and rights violations under British rule.

Ahilyabai's approach to solve the same problem stands as a lesson for the world. By addressing the root causes of crime and offering opportunities for reform and integration, Ahilyabai had solved a pressing law and order issue and with it uplifted entire communities. Her policies were humane and effectives. Her approach to conflict management and social integration remains a valuable lesson in governance, demonstrating that compassion and understanding can be more effective than punitive measures in creating a harmonious and prosperous society.

WATER MANAGEMENT

Ahilyabai Holkar's approach to water management was as much a matter of governance as a reflection of her deep spiritual connection to nature. Her daily worship of river sands from the Ganga, Yamuna, Saraswati, Godavari, Kshipra, and Narmada symbolized her reverence for life-giving streams. This spiritual foundation formed the basis of her practical approach to water conservation and management throughout her realm.

The ancient wisdom from the Matsya Purana resonated in Ahilyabai's actions:

"एवं निरुदके देशे यः कूपं कारयेद्बुधः ।

बिन्दौ बिन्दौ च तोयस्य वसेत्संवत्सरं दिवि ॥"

One who builds a well where water is scarce, gains puṇya. Equipped with that puṇya, he gets to live in swarga for as many years as the drops of water in the well!

Ahilyabai took this teaching to heart, embarking on an ambitious program of water infrastructure development that would benefit generations to come.

Her water management strategy was comprehensive, encompassing:

- **Lakes**: Ahilyabai constructed lakes at multiple locations, designed to capture both spring water and rainwater. The Malhar Lake near Jejuri, spanning 18 acres, and lakes at Trimbakeshwar, Omkareshwar, and along the Indore-Maheshwar highway stand as testaments to her foresight.

- **Wells:** Hundreds of wells were constructed across her realm and beyond, from Chandwad to Kashi. These wells, often adorned with architectural elements like stone arches and deity niches, serving both practical and spiritual purposes.

- **Kunda** (Tanks): Ahilyabai commissioned the construction of numerous Kunda near temples. These stone tanks with steps on all four sides provide easy access to water for devotees.

- **Water Management**: The Malhar Lake at Jejuri exemplifies Ahilyabai's sophisticated approach to water management. This system, which includes the lake, supplementary wells, underground channels, and tanks within the town, demonstrates a holistic understanding of water use and reuse.

Separate channel of river was used for washing clothes and utensils this ensured that drinking water was not contaminated. Additionally grey water was diverted for irrigation.

Ahilyabai's water works were characterized by:

- Sustainability: Her projects were designed to last, with many still functioning today.

- Holistic Approach: She addressed various water needs, from agriculture to religious rituals.

- Innovation: The use of underground channels and gray water recycling in Jejuri showcase her forward-thinking approach.

- Widespread Impact: Her projects extended to pilgrimage sites across India.

In places where water scarcity was a constant threat, Ahilyabai's initiatives provided a lifeline for countless communities. Her approach to water management focused on ensuring long-term water security.

In today's context of increasing water scarcity and climate change, Ahilyadevi's integrated approach to water conservation and management offers valuable lessons.

TREE PLANTATION INITIATIVES

Ahilyabai's tree plantation initiatives reflect a deep understanding of ecological balance and spiritual significance, as echoed in the Bhavishya Purana:

अश्वत्थमेकं पिचुमंदमेकं न्यग्रोधमेकं दश चिञ्चिणीकान् ।

कपित्थबिल्वामलकीत्रयं च पञ्चाम्रवापी नरकं न पश्येत् ।।

He who plants one Peepal, Neem and Banyan tree; ten Tamarind and three each of Bel and Amala trees and five trees of Mango goes to heaven.

Ahilyabai's tree planting initiatives were comprehensive and far-reaching:

1. Roadside Plantations: She lined roads with shady trees, providing comfort to travelers and enhancing the aesthetic appeal.

2. Temple Surroundings: Recognizing the spiritual significance of certain trees, she encouraged their plantation around temples, creating serene and sacred spaces.

3. Water Bodies: Trees were planted along ponds and rivers. This helps in preventing soil erosion and maintaining water quality.

4. Pilgrimage Routes: Fruit-bearing trees were strategically planted along pilgrimage routes, offering sustenance to weary travelers.

5. Floral Gardens: Flower beds were established near temples creating employment and also ensuring a steady supply of flowers for worship.

6. Agricultural Initiatives: Ahilyabai urged farmers to plant and nurture 20 saplings each, including: Peepal, Bel, Banyan, and fruit-bearing trees such as: Mango, Amla, Tamarind, Guava, and Ber.

7. Tribal Welfare: She encouraged tribal communities to plant trees for food, firewood and fodder.

8. Conservation Measures: Under her rule, unauthorized felling of trees was a punishable offense.

Ahilyabai's approach to tree plantation was holistic and addressed multiple needs including – environmental, economic, spiritual, social, and aesthetic.

In today's context of climate change and environmental degradation, Devi's green initiatives offer valuable lessons. Her approach demonstrates how traditional wisdom can be applied to address modern challenges.

INFRASTRUCTURE DEVELOPMENT

Devi Ahilyabai Holkar's approach to infrastructure development was as visionary as it was compassionate. Her personal pilgrimages to sites like Pandharpur, Mathura, and Kashi provided her with firsthand insight into the challenges faced by pilgrims. This experience fueled her determination to transform the pilgrimage experience across India.

Roads and Bridges:

Through her tireless efforts, Ahilyabai made pilgrimage possible to more and more devotees from all walks of life. Here are some of the roads she built -

- A road from Kolkata to Kashi
- A bridge on Karmanashini river, Bengal
- Repaired the Trimbakeshwar Bridge, Nasik.
- Mosam Bridge, Malegaon, which is still in use.

These projects facilitated travel and also boosted trade and communication across regions.

Dharmashalas:

Ahilyabai established numerous Dharmashalas at pilgrimage sites across the country including those at - Badrinath, Kedarnath, Haridwar, Kashi, Ayodhya, Gaya, Naimisharanya, Amarkantak, Ujjain, Omkareshwar, Nasik, Bhimashankar, and Rameshwar, among others. Many of these rest houses have faithfully served generations of pilgrims.

These Dharmashalas provided safety and lodging facility for weary travellers in the spiritual journeys. Constructed predominantly with brick, these rest houses were surrounded by tall walls for security. At each Dharmashala, a Shivalinga was installed and the courtyard was adorned by a Tulsi Vrindavan to create a spiritual atmosphere.

Strategically located on the banks of rivers or near wells, these rest houses were provided with easy access to water. Ahilyabai initiated *Anna-chhatra* at most of the sites to ensure food security. To oversee the maintenance and operations of these facilities, Ahilyabai employed dedicated staff members and allocated funds or village revenues to ensure their sustainability.

Ghats:

Ahilyabai undertook the construction of numerous Ghats, including Nagaghat at Paithan on the Godavari river, ghats on the Godavari at Nasik and Puntambe, 28 ghats on the Narmada at Maheshwar, and the renowned Manikarnika and Dash-Ashwamedh ghats on the Ganga at Kashi. She also built ghats at Ayodhya, Mathura, Haridwar, Prayag, Ujjain, Pushkar and other sacred sites. These ghats facilitated religious rituals, improved access to river and provided for a connection to the other bank.

Ahilyabai's infrastructure projects improved pilgrimage accessibility. She focused on addressing the basic needs of pilgrims by ensuring safe travel, providing rest points, and ensuring access to water and food. That many of her structures are still in use today, speak of their quality. Her infrastructure projects connected various parts of India.

TOWN PLANNING

After Ahilyabai moved to Maheshwar though she built for herself a humble house in the fort, she developed the town in every way possible. Near the Maheshwar fort, there used to be an old market. She settled a colony of weavers over there. She established new markets and neighbourhoods such as - Aditwar Peth, Mangalwar Peth, Phansephura, Govindpura, Malharganj etc.

Businessmen from nearby villages were encouraged to settle in Maheshwar, and commercial sectors were constructed. Various incentives were provided to traders to enhance commerce and industry. Skilled artisans were invited from various parts of India to Maheshwar to start textile production. Ahilyabai saw to it that the weavers were provided with resources and ensured their welfare. Maheshwari sarees made here became famous across India, contributing significantly to the textile industry.

She built Sanskrit schools in Maheshwar. She restored old temples, creating employment opportunities around them for flower sellers, artists, carpenters, architects, priests, cooks and others. The chanting of Vedas and the smoke of holy fire again rose from Maheshwar.

Ahilyabai rendered great service to Marathi literature by giving patronage to many poets and writers. The famous Marathi poet Moropant, who wrote a 108 different Ramayana, came to Maheshwar on hearing Ahilyabai's fame. He received great respect at her court. Sanskrit scholars such as Khushali Ram received her patronage.

When singer Ananta Fandi of Sangamner, went to Maheshwar, Devi rewarded him richly. Fandi was famous for writing Lavani, a form of romantic poetry. When he presented his art in her court, it is said, that Ahilya Devi praised his skills but also advised him to use his poetic talent for singing kirtan, the glories of god. Then on he started to perform Kirtan. Later his son, Sawai Fandi also became a Kirtankar.

Ahilyabai honored scholars, writers, poets, Harikatha singers and Kirtankars with rich clothes and awards. She rewarded not only learned men but men of arms as well. For example an entry from 1791 account book tells – On the Chaitra Shuddha Pratipada (New Year Day) - 11 learned Brahmins, 78 officers with their clerks, and 31 Shiledars were honored with dresses and gifts.

Just as Dhara Nagari had become a hub for scholars during the reign of Raja Bhoj, Maheshwar emerged as a city of scholars during the rule of Ahilyabai.

4. HEALING A WOUNDED CIVILIZATION

Let us examine a present-day wounded civilization and the efforts being taken to heal it. It is the once the prosperous and peaceful land of Gandhar, now Afghanistan. It was adorned with Hindu, Buddhist, Parsee, and Greek temples. No nation can understand the consequences of losing its culture better than Afghanistan, which lost its heritage to invasions, wars, and terrorism.

Today, under Taliban, its culture has been suppressed, where singing is forbidden, children aren't allowed to fly kites, films are banned, and the world's largest Buddha statues are reduced to rubble. It has become a country without a cultural identity. Ironically, the plaque outside its National Museum reads, "A nation stays alive when its culture stays alive."

Paul Smith, a former British Council Country Director for Afghanistan, proposed several strategies to rejuvenate the nation. He emphasized the importance of establishing robust pillars of governance, development, security, and, most crucially, its own culture. He further suggested– "to revive its culture and to secure its future, the country should rebuild the colossal statues of the Bamiyan Buddhas."

Ahilyabai focused on all four pillars: governance, development, security, and culture. Preserving culture begins with safeguarding the idols of deities and their homes, the temples. Remarkably ahead of her time, Ahilyabai anticipated a concept now widely recognized in the 21st century. Through her temple reconstruction efforts she was contributing to keeping the culture alive, and thereby keeping the nation alive.

When Ahilyabai Holkar ascended to power, she inherited not just a kingdom, but a civilization in distress. For over five centuries, the Indic civilization had endured relentless attacks, resulting in widespread destruction and cultural trauma. The landscape was scarred by ruins of temples and Universities. The arts and sciences were in sharp decline and poverty was on the rise.

In this bleak scenario, Ahilyabai's reign marked the beginning of a cultural and spiritual renaissance, with temple reconstruction at its core. Her holistic approach to rebuild the civilization included -

1. **Temple Reconstruction**:
   By rebuilding temples, she restored places of worship that became centers of community life, learning, and cultural preservation.

2. **Support for Art and Architecture**:
   Her patronage revived traditional art forms and architectural styles, preserving centuries-old knowledge and skills.

3. **Establishment of Schools**:
   Recognizing the importance of education, she founded schools, rekindling the flame of learning that had been dimmed by years of conflict.

4. **Honoring Scholars and Storytellers**:
   By supporting these custodians of culture, she ensured the continuation and revival of oral traditions and literature.

ROLE OF TEMPLES

Ahilyabai understood that temples were more than just religious structures; they were the cornerstones of Indic civilization. Their roles were multifaceted:

1. **Spiritual Centers:** Temples provided a sacred space for worship, rituals, and spiritual discourses.

2. **Community Hubs:** Temples served as gathering places for festivals and other events, fostering social cohesion.

3. **Educational Institutions:** Many temples functioned as Pathashalas (schools), teaching subjects ranging from Sanskrit to Mathematics.

4. **Cultural Preservers:** Temples were patrons of arts, maintained libraries of manuscripts and also provided a stage for music, dance and drama performances.

5. **Economic Engines:** Temple towns became centers of commerce, attracting pilgrims and creating markets for local crafts.

6. **Social Welfare Centers:** Many temples ran hospitals, operated Anna-chhatra, and offered halls for celebrating important life events like weddings.

7. **Agricultural Innovators:** Some temples helped in building irrigation systems and in preserving indigenous grain varieties through specific offering requirements.

8. **Dispute Resolution Centers:** Some temples played a role in maintaining law and order within their jurisdictions.

9. **Animal Welfare Centers:** Many temples maintained Goshala (cow shelters) and some even cared for elephants, preserving elephant training practices.

By rebuilding temples, Ahilyabai was reviving entire ecosystems of knowledge, culture, and community support.

EFFECTS OF TEMPLE DESTRUCTION

The destruction of temples by invading forces was not merely an act of architectural demolition; it was a systematic assault on the very fabric of Indian civilization. These acts of destruction were often accompanied by a horrifying array of atrocities:

- Sacred idols, revered for centuries, were defaced or destroyed.
- Those who attempted to defend their sacred spaces were brutally killed.
- The custodians of spiritual and cultural knowledge were often targeted.
- Surrounding shops and homes were razed, displacing entire populations.
- The looting of temple treasures, including deity's gold ornaments and other valuable items.

Sita Ram Goel's meticulous documentation in "*Hindu Temples: What Happened to Them*" provides a sobering glimpse into the extent of this destruction. His list of about three thousand destroyed temples across India is, by his own admission, merely the tip of the iceberg. Estimates suggest that the total number of temples destroyed during this period could run into tens of thousands.

The impact of a single temple's destruction reverberates far beyond its immediate vicinity:

1. **Spiritual Damage:** The loss of a sacred space severs the community's connection to its spiritual heritage, leaving a void.

2. **Cultural Loss:** Temples were also repositories of art, literature, and traditional knowledge. Their destruction resulted in an irretrievable loss of local customs, art forms, technical skills, and cultural practices.

3. **Economic Impact:** The temple economy supported a vast network of artisans, performers, and small businesses. Its destruction led to widespread unemployment and economic distress.

4. **Psychological Trauma:** The repeated destruction of temples instilled a deep-seated fear in the Hindu population. This fear was so profound that even when opportunities for rebuilding arose, many were too traumatized to act.

The case of Somnath temple illustrates the long-lasting impact of the fear instilled by continuous attacks. It took nearly 80 years after Aurangzeb's death, for the worship to resume at the site. And even after that long time, when Ahilyabai Holkar rebuilt the temple, she placed the deity on a lower floor, as a precautionary measure against potential future attacks.

This fear of serial destruction created a society living in constant apprehension. The task of rebuilding was thus not limited to physical level it involved healing psychological wounds as well.

In this context, Ahilyabai's work was enkindling hope, reviving cultural practices, and helping a traumatized society reclaim its spiritual and cultural heritage.

RESILIENCE IN ADVERSITY

The Hindu community, including Jains, Buddhists, and Sikhs, demonstrated remarkable resilience in the face of the attacks on their faith. Their coping strategies were diverse and multifaceted:

1. **Armed Resistance:**
Not only kings and citizens, even monks took up arms to defend their sacred spaces. A notable example is the 1664 battle where Naga Sadhus defeated Aurangzeb's forces attacking the Kashi Vishvanath temple.

2. **Flight and Preservation:**
Meenakshi Jain's book *"Flight Of Deities and Rebirth of Temples"* details the extraordinary measures taken to protect sacred idols. In the north, priests carried idols from Uttar Pradesh to Rajput kingdoms for safekeeping. In South India, devotees sought refuge in Kerala with their deities. Upon coming to know of an impending attack, devotees buried the idols of their beloved Devatas or submerged them in rivers for protection. Ingenious methods were employed to protect the

idols such as - at Meenakshi temple the main murti was replaced with a duplicate; at Chidambaram idols were disguised as corpses and moved to safety. The idol of Sri Ranganath was moved to Tirupati, while Sri Vitthala murti was moved from Pandharpur to Vijaynagar. In Goa, to escape Portuguese destruction, Hindus shifted idols from South to North Goa.

3. Spiritual Revitalization:

During this onslaught, spiritual leaders played a crucial role in re-establishing Dharma. Krishna devotees revitalized the Mathura-Braj region in the 15th and 16th centuries. Vallabhacharya, the founder of Pushti Marg, re-established Krishna worship in Gokul. Chaitanya Mahaprabhu rediscovered sacred sites associated with Krishna-Leela in Vrindavan. A pilgrimage route along these sites was revived. Through this people were able to state their right to the sacred landscape. Narayan Bhatt kept Kashi Vishvanath traditions alive, even in the absence of the temple.

All over India, Sanskrit works such as Ramayana, Mahabharata and Bhāgvat Purana were translated into regional languages, thereby facilitating and propagating the teachings of Hindu dharma. In the absence of temples, and the idols of deities, saints preached Nirgun Bhakti (formless devotion).

4. Temple Reconstruction:

During periods of relative calm, efforts were made to rebuild destroyed temples. Marathas and the Rajputs rebuilt temples in Mathura and Vrindavan. Notable reconstructions include the Somnath temple and Kashi Vishvanath temple. These efforts involved Sadhus, merchants, kings and queens, showcasing community-wide commitment to preservation.

Indeed, the Hindu community survives because at all the times there was some king, some monk or some citizen fighting for Dharma. Ahilyabai stands out as a shining example of this resilience.

The multifaceted response to adversity - combining armed resistance, preservation of deities, spiritual innovation, reconstruction efforts, and the emergence of leaders like Ahilyabai - demonstrates the incredible Hindu resilience. It is a testament to the enduring spirit of a civilization that refused to be erased and found new ways to preserve its core values.

TEMPLE RECONSTRUCTION

The ancient Puranas extol the virtues of jeernoddhar — maintenance, repair, restoration, renovation, and reconstruction of old temples, wells, and ponds:

वापी कूप तड़ागेषु देवतायतनेषु च।
जीर्णान्युद्धरते यस्तु पुण्यमष्ट गुणं भवेत।

Whosoever carries out the repairs of wells, lakes, and temples gains eight times more punya than the one who built it.

Inspired by these teachings, kings, queens, merchants, and the wealthy have historically and continuously contributed to building and reconstructing sacred structures.

After the fall of grand dynasties like the Pratihars, Pala, Yadava, Hoysala, Kakatiya etc. the temple-building tradition fell into decline. For centuries together grand temples had ceased to be built. The Birla Temple in Delhi that was constructed in 1933 by Ghanashyamdas Birla, marked the city's first significant temple built after nearly eight centuries. This ancient city of Indraprastha, founded by Krishna and the Pandavas, was in a state of such doom.

With the rise of Vijayanagar in the South and later the Marathas in Deccan, history took a new turn. Beginning with Rajmata Jijabai who rebuilt temples in Pune, was followed by Ch. Shivaji, and later Ch. Sambhaji who continued the practice of rebuilding temples. Among the Maratha ministers and sardars - Nanasaheb Peshwa built the Trimbakeshwar temple and Raghuji Bhosale rebuilt the Ramagiri temple. In this line came Ahilya Devi, who ushered in a new age of temple building. Her efforts brought architectural revival and breathed new life into an eternal civilization.

Ahilyabai's temple construction is a testament to her vision and dedication to Dharma. She repaired temples that had fallen into ruin or had been deliberately destroyed. Her work spanned all across India in regional architectural styles, nurturing diverse schools of architecture and fostering a new generation of Indian architects, builders and artists.

As a ruler devoted to spiritual service (Seva), Ahilyabai neither taxed nor controlled the temples that she restored. Her contributions were acts of devotion aimed at preserving cultural heritage.

Govindapant Ganu, a minister to Ahilyabai, was in charge of the Khasgi. All the charitable institutions and endowments of the Devi were under his management and supervision. The sites selected for temples and ghats, their architectural finish, the rules and regulations made for worship and festivals, all originated with him. Ahilyabai had appointed a scholar with excellent character, well-versed in Shastra, who was respected by the learned for her *Bhagirathi project.*

Ahilyabai's temple reconstruction project of bringing the Sanskriti-Ganga (life giving river of culture) to the Earth, were akin to ancient King Bhagiratha's monumental task of bringing the Celestial Ganga to the Earth.

Ahilyabai's efforts in temple reconstruction were complemented by initiatives in education, arts, and social welfare. She must have known that true healing required addressing the physical and cultural destruction. Her reign marked the beginning of a cultural and spiritual renaissance. By rebuilding temples and supporting their multifaceted roles, she laid the foundation for the revival of a civilization that had been pushed to the brink. Her legacy lives on in the physical structures as well as in the renewed spirit of a people who, under her leadership, began to reclaim their cultural identity and heritage.

The 12 Jyotirlingas, revered Shiva shrines scattered across India, hold a special place in Hindu spirituality. Ahilyabai's efforts to restore and revitalize these sites were nothing short of monumental. Her work touched all 12 sites, effectively re-establishing a sacred geography that had been disrupted. Her work is seen at all 12 sites:

- **Somnath, Gujarat**: In a dream vision revealing the location of the original Shivalinga within a mosque's ruins, Ahilyabai acted decisively. She retrieved the Shivalinga and constructed a modest two-story temple near the original site.

- **Vishwanath, Uttar Pradesh:** In 1777, Ahilyabai acquired land near the original site and built a small temple for Kashi Vishwanath.

- **Mallikarjun, Andhra Pradesh:** During Nizam's rule when the temple was in disrepair, Ahilyabai rebuilt it on a mountain top with steps leading down to the Krishna River.

- **Omkareshwar, Madhya Pradesh:** She restored this temple to its former glory after centuries of neglect.

- **Vaijnath, Maharashtra:** Ahilyabai rebuilt the temple that was in Nizam's territory. It had fallen into ruins due to lack of centuries of neglect.

- **Ghirishneshwar, Maharashtra:** Ahilyabai completed the reconstruction of the temple that had been started by her mother-in-law Gautamabai.

- **Trimbakeshwar, Maharashtra:** This temple was rebuilt by Nanasaheb Peshwa. Ahilyabai contributed towards developing its infrastructure.

- **Nagnath, Maharashtra:** Ahilyabai arranged annual payments for worship at Aundha Nagnath.

- **Mahakaleshwar, Madhya Pradesh**: Arranged for regular worship by the Holkar family on Mahashivratri.

Either Ahilyabai or her successors, established Annachhatra at the three other Jyotirlinga –**Rameshwar** in Tamil Nadu, **Gokarna** in Karnataka and at **Bheema-Shankar in Maharashtra**

Ahilyabai's reconstruction efforts stand as a testament to her commitment to preserving spiritual heritage.

SAPTAPURI AND CHAR DHAM

The Saptapuri and Char Dham are important places on India's spiritual landscape. They draw pilgrims from every corner of the subcontinent. These seven ancient cities and four sacred abodes found in Ahilyabai Holkar a devotee and a restorer. Her works stand at all of these sites that are stretched across the length and breadth of India.

In each of these seven cities, Ahilyabai left her indelible mark:

1. **Ayodhya**: The birthplace of Lord Rama blossomed under her care. She erected temples to Rama, Treta Rama, Bhairava, and Nageshwar. The Sharayu Ghat, Anna-chhatra, and a Dharmashala.

2. **Mathura**: Krishna's playground saw the construction of the Chain Bihari Mandir, two ghats on the Yamuna and a Dharmashala for devotees.

3. **Maya (Haridwar):** The gateway to the Himalayas received the Kushavarta Ghat and a Dharmashala from Ahilyabai's benevolence.

4. **Kashi (Varanasi):** Already detailed in her work at the 12 Jyotirlinga, Kashi found renewed glory under her patronage.

5. **Kanchi**: Ahilyabai arranged for the annual dispatch of Ganga water to this southern city.

6. **Avantika** (Ujjain): Here, a cluster of temples sprouted under her patronage - Lila-Purushottam, Janardan, Balaji, and Ganpati Mandir, along with a Dharmashala.

7. **Dwarka**: Krishna's western abode received an Anna-chhatra, ensuring no pilgrim went hungry.

The Char Dham or the four cardinal points of pilgrimage also received Ahilyabai's patronage:

1. **Badrinath**: A network of Dharmashalas at Rangad Chatti, Bedar Chatti, Vyas Ganga, Tanga-Nath, and Pawali provided rest to weary travelers. At Deva

Prayag, she created a verdant garden, a grazing field for cows, and various Kunda (water reservoirs), including the Gauri-Kunda and hot-water Kunda.

2. **Dwarka**: As mentioned in the Saptapuri.

3. **Rameshwaram**: Detailed in her work on the Jyotirlinga.

4. **Jagannath Puri:** Here, she built the Shree Ramchandra Mandir, accompanied by an Annachhatra and a garden.

Ahilyabai's patronage knew no sectarian bounds. While her Shiva Bhakti led her to rebuild numerous Shiva temples, including those dedicated to Malhari or Khandoba (the kuladevata of the Holkar family), she embraced the entire pantheon. Temples to Rama, Krishna, Vitthala, Hanuman, Balaji, and Devi sprouted across the land, a testament to her inclusive spirituality.

Her patronage extended to diverse spiritual traditions that had blossomed from the Vedic roots - the Nath Sampradaya, Mahanubhava Panth, Varakari Panth, Ramadasi Panth, Ganapatya Sampradaya, and Datta Sampradaya. From Chinchwad to Kolhapur, from Jamgaon's Swami Ramadas Monastery to Pushkar's Ganesh temple, Ahilyabai's benevolence knew no bounds.

In this grand endeavor of restoration and patronage, Ahilyabai Holkar did more than rebuild temples and establish Dharmashalas. She rekindled the flickering spiritual flame. Each restored site was a reaffirmation of India's timeless spiritual heritage.

At heart Ahilyabai was the queen of entire Bharat. Her patronage of holy sites across India revealed a national perspective that encompassed the entire subcontinent. She was not merely the queen of Malwa, but a Chakravarti - one whose temple-building chariot rolled unobstructed across the land, turning the wheel of Dharma.

REVITALIZING THE TEMPLE ECONOMY

In the Post-Mughal era, Ahilyabai Holkar emerged as a visionary architect of spiritual renewal. Her efforts to rejuvenate religious tourism were not mere acts of devotion, but a carefully orchestrated symphony of development that touched every aspect of the pilgrim's journey.

Ahilyabai must have understood that a temple alone did not make a pilgrimage. She built around it the infrastructure that would cradle the faith of millions:

- Roads unfurled like ribbons to connect sacred sites and make pilgrimage easier.

- Wells sprang up along these routes as sources of hydration.

- Trees were planted to offer shade and fruits to weary travelers.

- Dharmashalas rose at strategic locations to provide shelter.

- Anna-Chhatras were established to take care of pilgrim's hunger.

Through these initiatives, Ahilyabai touched every aspect of the pilgrim's experience. This must have been nothing short of a renaissance in religious tourism.

The flow of pilgrims along these revitalized routes, must have brought with them not just devotion, but commerce. Local artisans must have found new markets for their crafts, turning the wheel of prosperity.

Ahilyabai may have engineered a spiritual and economic revival that rippled across the subcontinent. In Ahilyabai Holkar, we see not only a temple builder but a master architect of spiritual and economic renewal, whose blueprint for revival is still relevant.

NETWORK OF SANCTUARY

In the tumultuous landscape of those days, temple towns stood as islands of refuge for Hindu resilience. A glimpse of this hidden network of support can be seen Ch. Shivaji Maharaj's daring escape from Agra in 1666. In disguise and with few loyal men, he moved from one sacred site to another - Mathura, Prayag, Kashi, Gaya, Puri - each temple town offered him physical sanctuary till he reached Raigad. In Mathura, the cradle of Krishna's legends, young Sambhaji Raje was sheltered by a Brahmin family for months before his return to Raigad. These were not mere pit stops on a journey, but vital links in a chain of Hindu solidarity that stretched across the subcontinent.

About a century before Ahilyabai, Ramadas Swami had built numerous temples dedicated to SriRama and

Hanuman. His influence extended far and wide as he and his disciples founded hundreds of monasteries stretching from Badrinath in the north to those in Rajasthan, Madhya Pradesh, Andhra Pradesh, Maharashtra, and Karnataka. These religious centers were not merely places of worship; but are believed to have served as a sophisticated intelligence network for the Hindavi Swarajya.

Surely this must not have escaped Ahilyabai's keen eye. A strategist and a devotee, she must have recognized the profound importance of the sacred spaces. Her mission to fortify these bastions of belief should also be considered from the perspective that - each temple doubled as a Hindu sanctuary in lands often ruled by those hostile to the faith.

She built temples and allocated resources to ensure their economic sustainability. She built fortified walls around the Dharmashalas for security. She created havens that would support pilgrims, locals, travelers and the Hindus in distress.

Through her works Ahilyabai had weaved a network of Hindu solidarity across the subcontinent. For Hindus living under hostile rule, these spaces offered a glimpse of freedom, a taste of cultural autonomy, and a reminder of their shared heritage.

By investing in these centers of communal strength Ahilyabai was preserving the very soul of Hindu civilization. Her fortification of this Hindu support system stands as a masterclass in cultural preservation and community building. She created a network of sanctuary and solidarity transcended political boundaries. She knew that true strength did not lie in armies alone, but in the unbreakable bonds of shared belief and mutual support in the community.

VISION OF A UNITED BHARAT

The ancient Vishnu Purana defines the geographical expanse of Bharat as:

उत्तरं यत् समुद्रस्य हिमाद्रेश्चैव दक्षिणम् |
वर्षं तद् भारतं नाम भारती यत्र सन्ततिः ||

The land mass that lies to the north of the ocean and to the south of the great Himalayan range is the land called Bharat. There dwell the descendants of Bharata.

This vision of a unified Bharat, stretching from the Himalayas to the seas, found its champion in Ahilyabai Holkar. Her efforts towards national integration were deeply rooted in the spiritual and cultural fabric of the land.

The Puranas, through their Sthan-mahatmya, had long sown the seeds of national unity by praising thousands of sacred sites scattered across the subcontinent - from Peshawar to Dhaka, from Kashmir to Sri Lanka and from Baluchistan to Tibet. This spiritual geography transcended the political boundaries to create a sense of a cultural Bharata.

This sense of unity is seen in below sample acts concerning the Kashi Vishvanath temple –

1. In the late 13th century, when pilgrims to Kashi were required to pay Jiziya tax, the Hoysala Em-

peror, Sri Narasimha III, who was Jain by faith, granted the revenues of Hebbale village for his citizen's pilgrimage. A part of it went towards the maintenance of the Vishvanath temple.

2. When the temple was destroyed it was rebuilt at different times by a Sadhu and Rajput Todarmal, then by a Gujarati merchant and lastly by Devi Ahilyabai.

3. The temple's spire was plated in gold by a Sikh Raja Ranjit Singh.

   A Sikh, a Jain, a Hindu, a South Indian, a North Indian, a West Indian, a King, a Queen, a Sadhu ... all of them were united by their devotion to Kashi Vishwanath. It speaks of only one thing - the religious, cultural and geographical unity of India.

Consider Ahilyabai's initiative of annual offering of Ganga waters for abhishek (ritual bath for deity) at various Shiva temples:

- South: Rameshwaram, Mallikarjun, Gokarna Mahabaleshwar

- West: Panchavati, Trimbakeshwar, Bheema-Shankar, Somnath, Dwaraka, Nathadwar

- East: Mahakaleshwar, Rajarajeshwar, Vaijanath

- North: Badri Kedareshwar, Kashi Vishvanath, Pashupatinath

This was not merely a religious act. Ahilyabai in a profound gesture of national integration was connecting diverse regions through the sacred waters of Ganga.

Ahilyabai's ghats not only facilitated religious rituals, but they also offered a place to park and board a boat, thereby connecting the two banks of the river. Her ghats, roads and bridges were connecting different parts of India – spiritually, culturally and geographically.

The significance of Ahilyabai's efforts becomes even more apparent when contrasted with later British policies. Beginning in 1803 British built a customs line that ran from Bengal to Punjab. It partitioned India into – the landlocked North that was far from salt sources and the coastal areas where salt was produced. This customs line was a thorny hedge that stood up to 12 feet tall and up to 14 feet wide. This "Great Hedge of India" ran almost 4,000 km long. At its peak, 12,000 people were employed to patrol the line and run the customs posts along it. It collected Salt-Tax in Millions of Rupees, while preventing free trade and travel; thereby disconnecting Indians from the land and each other.

I recognize this as - while Ahilyabai sought to connect and empower, the British aim was to disconnect and control.

Ahilyabai's efforts were preserving the past and at the same time building a foundation for a united future.

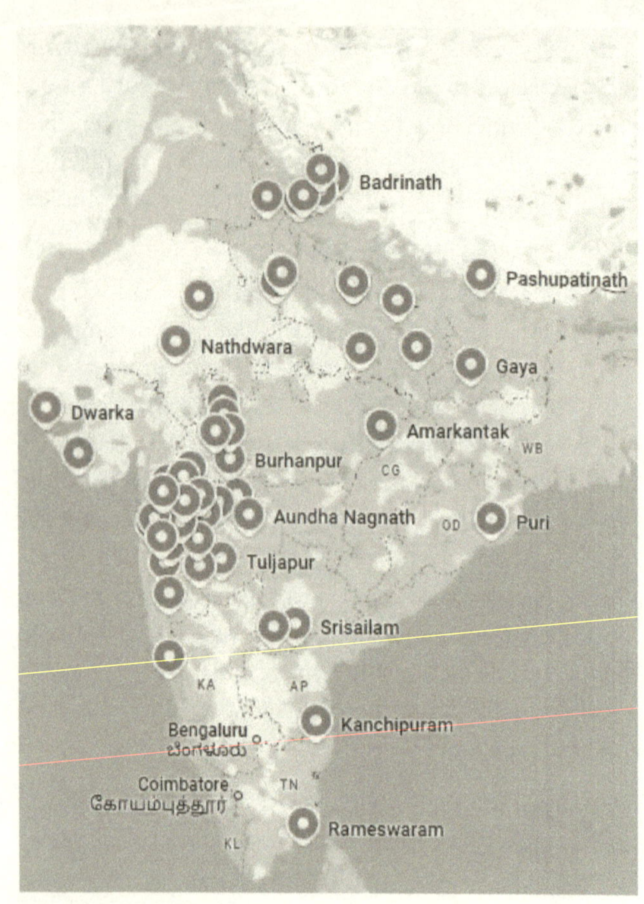

THE FOOTPRINT OF AHILYABAI'S WORK

5. DEVI'S PERSONAL LIFE

The learned Pandit Khushaliram Bhatta was summoned to the court of Ahilyabai, his mind a repository of ancient lore. Before him sat Devi Ahilyabai herself; not as a ruler demanding a work singing her praise; but as a seeker of knowledge, inviting him to write a book on Raj-Dharma.

Khushaliram wrote this book on Dharma Shastra, and called it Ahalya-Kamadhenu. Completed in 1771, its 1500 pages encompass the duties of rulers. Like the celestial wish-fulfilling cow, this Kamadhenu promises to nourish the realm with the milk of wisdom. Each chapter, called a Vatsa or calf, represents an aspect of governance or ritual. Within its pages, one finds knowledge of ancient texts:

- Rituals for each tithi (lunar day) of the month
- Samskara, or rites that mark the journey of life
- The ritual of temple visitation and deity worship
- The principles of Vastu Rachana or architecture.
- The veneration of life-giving rivers

The Ahalya-Kamadhenu also documents the lineage of Holkars, and some accounts of Devi's charity.

The Ahalya-Kamadhenu serves multiple purposes: It is a guide for future leaders and a repository of traditional rituals and practices. In a way this work is a symbol of cultural revival representing the resurgence of Sanskrit learning and Hindu traditions. This work remains relevant today for leaders to achieve political success and dharmic fulfillment and for the common as a roadmap on how to be a practicing Hindu.

The concept of *Pancha-Rina* or the five debts is deeply embedded in the Hindu Dharma. It is a grand scheme that connects one to all living and non-living beings. These debts are owed to traditional knowledge, Devatas, nature, ancestors & descendants, community, and animals. From these debts emerges the *Panch-Maha-Yajna* or the five great acts of giving back that bind individual to society and mortal to divine.

In the average Hindu household, the simple act of feeding a student or a wandering pilgrim becomes a sacred rite. Though each contribution is small, like droplets in an ocean, together they formed a mighty current of compassion that sustained society.

Ahilyabai Holkar was an heir to this tradition but with the resources of a kingdom at her disposal. In her hands, the personal practice of Panch-Maha-Yajna became a grand symphony of social welfare.

Her daily routine included the Panch-Maha-Yajna:

- Dawn broke with the rustle of sacred texts, the Brahma Yajna of knowledge

- The sun climbed higher as she performed her puja, the Deva Yajna of devotion

- Mid-morning she fed the cow at her doorstep, the Bhut Yajna of animal service.

- At Midday she performed Anna-daan. She never had lunch alone; lunch was with family, ministers and staff, her Manushya Yajna.

- In the afternoon she went to the court for attending the routine state affairs. She worked in the court till the sunset.

- At sunset she performed her evening puja and ate some fruits. She would go the court again at 9 pm and work up to 11 pm. In this session she would read and dictate letters to be dispatched. After that she would retire for sleep.

Ahilyabai's Panch-Maha-Yajna extended far beyond personal level:

1. **Brahma Yajna** – service of knowledge:
   - Establishing Pathashala
   - Arranging communal Purana reciting sessions

2. **Deva Yajna** – service to the Divine:
   - Planting trees
   - Encouraging subjects to plant trees.

3. **Pitru Yajna** - service to Ancestors:
   - Honoring the legacy of those who came before
   - Protecting and preserving culture

4. **Manushya Yajna -** The service of Humanity:
   - Establishing Anna-chhatra to feed the hungry
   - Distributing blankets in winter
   - Storing grains for times of famine
   - Ensuring that prisoners too were well-fed
   - Building wells and tanks for water supply

5. **Bhuta Yajna** - The service of All Beings:
   - Allocating grazing grounds for cattle
   - Designating cornfields for birds
   - Providing flour balls for fish

By establishing enduring structures for education, charity, and environmental stewardship, Ahilyabai ensured that the Panch-Maha-Yajna* would continue long after her reign. Each Pathashala, each Annachhatra, each recitation of Purana perpetuated the cycle of giving.

Ahilyabai Holkar transformed her kingdom into a vast yajna-shala, a sacred space where every act of governance became an offering to the divine. Her reign exemplifies how ancient wisdom can be applied to elevate the society and how all forms of life can be nourished.

*The Panch-Maha-Yajna is not confined to the classical Sanskrit texts or to the elite. Indian folk songs and traditions too carry the same message of compassion towards all living beings. This Sohar song, from the collections of Smt. Malini Avasthi ji, for example, captures the Manushya and Bhoot Yajna. In a conversation Kausalya asks, "What virtue lies in planting mango trees and digging lakes?" Dasharatha replies, "One earns merit when the hungry travellers find sustenance in the mangoes, and when thirsty cows drink at the lakes."

कौसल्या - अमवा लगावे कौन फल मिलिये मोरे साहेब?
दशरथ - राही बाटे जौनो अमवा खईंये तब फल मिलिहै सुनहू।
कौसल्या - तलैय्या खनावे कौन फल मिलिये मोरे साहेब?
दशरथ - गंय्या पिवे जोणो पनिया तब फल मिलिहै सुनहू।

DEVI'S BRAHMA YAJNA

Ahilyabai's library was a treasure trove of ancient wisdom. Here were the Vedas and Upanishads - the foundation of eternal dharma; the epics - Ramayana and Mahabharata - unfolding their tales of heroism; and the Puranas retelling sacred geographies and ancient lores. Each text was carefully chosen to nourish the soul of a nation. The books included -

- Veda-Pothi and Upanishads: The fountainhead of Indian thought

- Valmiki Ramayana and Mahabharata: Epic narratives that shaped moral and cultural landscape

- Vishnu-Sahasra-Nama: 1,000 names of Vishnu

- Bhagavad-Gita: a guide for righteous living

- Dnyāneshwari: Geeta in the common tongue

- Bhāgvat Purana, Padma Purana: Repositories of devotion, geographies and histories

- Mathura and Yamuna Mahatmya: Sacred geographies, mapping the spiritual landscape

- Vaidya-Nidana: The art and science of healing

- Dana Chandrika: The guide to charity

- Puja Prakar: Rituals of worship

- Muhurta Chintamani: science of auspicious time

- Vapi Kupotsarga Prayoga: Art and science of well construction

- Malhari Kavacha: Protective mantra of Malhari.

- Nirnaya Sindhu Pothi: A guide to religious living

- Vishnu Pratishtha Padhati: The consecration of the divine, a manual for temple building

Each of these texts helped build Ahilyabai's vision for renewal. The Mathura and Yamuna Mahatmya, for instance, weren't mere descriptions of holy places; they were the blueprints for her ambitious temple and ghat construction projects. The Vapi Kupotsarga Prayoga guided her water management initiatives.

In the days before the printing press, Ahilyabai's patronage for making copies of ancient texts provided livelihood to scribes and helped preserve texts. She also gave away hand-written manuscripts as gifts to story-tellers.

As Ahilyabai listened to these texts from the Purohit, one can imagine the visions that must have danced before her eyes - of ancient temples rising anew, of sacred rivers flowing unimpeded, of a civilization reborn. Each rebuilt temple, each restored ghat, each act of charity was a manifestation of the wisdom contained in these sacred texts.

Ahilyabai's library was the heart beat of her reign, the wellspring from which flowed her vision of cultural and spiritual renewal. Through her devotion to these texts and her efforts to implement their teachings, Ahilyabai performed a grand Brahma Yajna that would revitalize an entire civilization.

Rulers are often remembered for their lavish palaces and valuable collections. But the Maratha rulers stand apart, as a beacon of simplicity. Ahilyabai too lived a simple life.

On one hand, Ahilyabai built across the length and breadth of India, temples that rose to skies. Their tall spires, ornate pillars and walls with intricate carvings and paintings became grand homes of the deities.

But, on the other hand, her own dwelling was a humble abode, built with wooden pillars and bricks. At the heart of this modest home lay the Puja-Ghar, and in the courtyard, stood a Tulsi Vrindavan, from where Ahilyabai took the darshan of Narmada Maiyya at dawn and dusk.

The true ornament of her house was not in the ostentatious display of wealth, but in the guests who visited her. Her home was not an isolated retreat; it was a way station for pilgrims on their journey to Kashi, where weary travelers found nourishment before continuing their journey.

The paradox of Ahilyabai's life extended to her very attire. As an architect of the flourishing Maheshwari saree industry, she could have draped herself in the finest silks, decorated with threads of gold. Instead, she chose the purity of a simple white saree.

Ahilyabai was living the Bhagvad Geeta's teaching of *Aparigrah* (a minimalistic lifestyle) -

योगी युञ्जीत सततमात्मानं रहसि स्थितः।
एकाकी यतचित्तात्मा निराशीरपरिग्रहः || 6.10 ||

A Yogi who has mastered control over his mind and body lives a life free from desires and the need for material possessions.

Her simplicity starkly contrasts with Bollywood's glittering depictions of royal courts, featuring magnificent halls, gem-encrusted thrones, heavy curtains, and royalty covered in silk and gold. The reality of Maratha courts, as observed by John Malcom, was far removed from such ostentation. Their lifestyle mirrored that of their subjects, bridging the often vast gulf between the ruler and the ruled.

This combination of grand public works and personal simplicity speaks of Ahilyabai's philosophy. She prioritized public welfare, directing resources towards projects that benefited her people. Her leadership demonstrated that true power lies not in accumulation, but in distribution. Also power lies not in living above one's people, but among them.

The court of Ahilyadevi

Ahlyadevi's home and the courtyard

The life of Ahilyabai Holkar, filled with achievements was also one that was marked with profound personal loss. Her journey through grief stands as a testament to her indomitable spirit and her commitment to dharma in the face of life's harsh trials.

The untimely death of her husband Khanderao, in her young age, was a blow that would have shattered a lesser spirit, but she made through it. Later the loss of her father-in-law and political guru, Subhedar Malhar Rao, left her without a trusted advisor. The passing of her only son was a cruel twist of fate that robbed her of her heir.

Yet, Ahilyabai grew stronger with each storm. Her daughter Muktabai and grandson Nathoba became wellsprings of joy in a life shadowed by loss. The marriage of Nathoba in 1780 brought new hope.

But fate, it seemed, was not done testing Ahilyabai's resolve. The death of Nathoba, in 1790 snatched away her plans for adoption and succession. Merely a year later, Muktabai's husband succumbed to illness. And in a final, heart-wrenching blow, Muktabai chose to follow her husband in sati, leaving Ahilyabai bereft of her last immediate family member.

The specter of sati loomed large over Ahilyabai's life. In her lifetime, she witnessed no less than seventeen women - wives and concubines of her male relatives - choose pyre over widowhood. This stark reality stands in contrast to some of the contemporary families; the Bhosale women like Jijabai, Yesubai, and Tarabai, and most of the Peshwa widows chose to live on after their husbands' deaths.

Muktabai's death struck Ahilyabai to her core. For days, she went without food in her grief. She later erected a Chhatri on the banks of the Narmada, a lasting monument to her beloved daughter.

As Ahilyabai's life neared its end, her thoughts were not on personal loss but on the future of her state and the larger Maratha confederacy. Even in her final moments, she remained unfazed by the fear of death. Just as she had stood steadfast after the passing of Malhar Rao and Malerao, she faced her own end with the same unwavering resolve, embodying the strength and composure of a true ruler.

Her final counsel to Tukojirao and other commanders resonates with the wisdom of a leader who had transcended personal ambition:

- She urged unity, warning against the corrosive power of internal enmity

- She emphasized the importance of nation-building over petty grievances

- She cautioned against letting local egos overshadow national interests

Even as her health failed, Ahilyabai's commitment to her daily routines of charity and service remained unshaken. On the fourteenth day of Shravan (August 13, 1795), with the name of Shiva on her lips, she quietly departed this world, leaving Maheshwar - and indeed all of India - in mourning.

In Ahilyabai, we see a ruler who was not defined by her losses, but by her response to them. Each tragedy, rather than diminishing her, seemed to fuel her commitment to her Dharma. Her final days, marked by wisdom and selfless concern for her state's future, stand as a fitting capstone to a life of extraordinary service and spiritual strength.

As the curtain fell on this glorious chapter of Indian history, Ahilyabai left behind grand monuments in stone and long lasting institutions of charity. Her legacy also includes lessons in spiritual resilience and selfless leadership. In her life and in her passing, she embodied the highest ideals of Hindu philosophy - detachment from personal sorrow, unwavering devotion to duty, and a vision that transcended the boundaries of her own existence to embrace the welfare of all.

6. THE ERA AFTER AHILYABAI

TIMELINE

1797:   Death of Tukojirao Holkar

1800:   Death of Nana Fadnavis

1775-1782:
   First Anglo-Maratha war
   Marathas win

1803:   Second Anglo-Maratha war
   British win Delhi from Marathas
   British build victory pillar at Noida

1818:   The Third Anglo-Maratha War
   British win this war
   The beginning of Colonial Rule in India
   British build victory pillar at Bhima-Koregaon

1857:   The First War of Independence

1947:   The Partition of India
   India gets independence

The passing of Ahilyabai in 1795 marked the beginning of a turbulent era that would see the fall of the grand Maratha power. As the sun set on the 18th century, it took with it a generation of Maratha stalwarts - Mahadji Scindia, Raghuji Angre, Ahilyabai Holkar, Peshwa Sawai Madhavrao and Nana Fadnavis - each a pillar of Maratha supremacy.

The Holkar house plunged into succession struggles after Tukojirao's death in 1797. Disputes between Holkars and Scindias that had began in the last years of Ahilyabai, worsened after her death. The Bhosale clan, already destabilized by earlier power struggles, found itself further weakened.

The Peshwa house too was rocked by power strife after the untimely death of Madhavrao Peshwa followed by the assassination of Peshwa Narayanrao. Nana Fadnavis had managed state affairs through a twelve-member regency council. He maintained the Maratha Confederacy amid internal conflicts and the rising power of the British East India Company. But the suicide of Sawai Madhavrao in 1795 followed by the death of Nana in 1800 marked the beginning of the end of the Maratha Empire.

These internal conflicts, like cracks in a mighty dam, weakened the Maratha forces from within. The ever opportunistic British saw their chance and struck. Marathas successfully defeated the British in the first Anglo-Maratha war. In the second war of 1803, British gained Delhi from the Marathas. Barely two decades after Ahilyabai's reign, the combined Maratha forces, were defeated in the third Anglo-Maratha war of 1818. With this defeat, the Hindavi Swarajya that had been nurtured by generations of Maratha leaders crumbled, and almost all of India fell under the shadow of the British East India Company.

The transformation was swift and brutal. Within 25 years of Ahilyabai's demise the Marathas, the Rajputs, the Wadiyars, the Nizam, various Nawabs - all were reduced to vassals of the British power. The subcontinent was now a patch work of over 600 Princely States and a vast British colony. The princely states were puppet regimes under the control of the British.

1857 WAR OF INDEPENDENCE

The 1857 war was India's desperate attempt to throw off the British yoke. It was led mainly by Marathas - Nanasaheb Peshwa, Tatya Tope, and the indomitable Rani Lakshmibai of Jhansi. The Rani died on the battlefield, Tatya was captured, tried and executed; while a defeated Nana Saheb fled and was never to be seen again.

The response of the Princely States to this war against the foreigners was mixed - some sheltered the freedom fighters, others remained neutral, while some even sided with the British.

The aftermath of this failed war was catastrophic. About 6,000 British were killed in this war. But after they emerged victorious they wiped out the revolutionaries brutally. P. N. Chopra in 'A comprehensive history of India' writes - in Oudh alone 1.5 Lakh Indians were killed, of which 1 Lakh were civilians. After British gained control over Delhi, over the next few months, mass hangings were seen along the Grand Trunk Road and revolutionaries were blown from the cannon. Hundreds of thousands of Indians were killed over the period of three years. By 1859 the revolt had died down.

In the wake of this carnage, India found herself firmly under the British heel, destined for another 90 years of colonial rule.

THE COLONIAL RULE

As the sun of Ahilyabai's era set, another dark night descended over India - the era of colonial rule. This period ushered in a different, yet equally devastating, form of assault on the temple institution that had been so painstakingly revived by leaders like Ahilyabai.

In Goa, under another European power, the Portuguese, the landscape was scarred by the razing of hundreds of Hindu temples. The ruins of these sacred structures often became the foundations for new churches, a stark symbol of cultural and religious subjugation. These physical attacks perpetuated a relentless cycle of desecration and displacement.

However, it was under British rule that the temples faced a far more insidious form of attack. While the structures often remained standing, the very soul of the temple institution was systematically dismantled:

1. **Educational Disruption:** The Pathashalas and Gurukuls associated with temples, which had been centers of learning for millennia, were disrupted.

2. **Cultural Erosion:** The vibrant traditions of music and dance, nurtured within temple precincts, were uprooted from their sacred context. The Devadasi tradition, attached to the temples, once respected as the bearer of arts, faced a heartbreaking decline. The status of Devadasi women was reduced to a point where they were unfairly labeled as prostitutes. The revered institution that had nurtured and preserved the rich heritage of Indian music and dance was completely dismantled, leaving behind a generation of helpless and disemployed Devadasis.

3. **Financial Strangulation:** Through various Religious Endowments Acts, temple finances and properties came under government control. This bureaucratic takeover took away the funds previously allocated for: local arts and crafts, Dharmashalas, Pathashalas, Goshala, Clinics and other community services.

Temples, that were centers of educational, social, cultural and spiritual activities, were reduced to mere places of worship. Their role was severely diminished. Along with this assault on the temple institution, the British simultaneously launched a cultural offensive that struck at the very heart of Indian civilization:

- **Language:** Sanskrit, the language of spirituality and science, was marginalized. Local dialects, the living voice of diverse communities, were downplayed.

- **Knowledge:** The Itihas and Puranas, repositories of Indian wisdom and cultural memory, were suppressed and ridiculed as mythologies. Indigenous knowledge systems, like the Ayurveda, Vatushastra, or Jyotishshastra were shrugged off as superstition. The Dharma Shastra, or ancient codes, were denigrated as misogynistic and casteist.
- **Technology:** Traditional industries, like - shipbuilding, metallurgy, steel, textiles etc., which were the backbone of local economies, were systematically dismantled.

This cultural colonization was comprehensive and far-reaching. English replaced Indian languages in administration and judiciary. The British education system, with its emphasis on rote learning and Western perspectives, supplanted the holistic Indian approach to knowledge. The concept of individual rights, central to the British constitution, overshadowed the dharmic focus on social responsibilities. While the wealth and knowledge of India fueled the Industrial Revolution; it ultimately led to mass-produced inexpensive British goods flooding the markets, replacing the handmade products of Indian cottage industries.

The colonial approach, while not physically destructive, was in many ways more insidious, striking at the very foundations of Indian culture and identity.

Ahilyabai came to power in the era after Mughals were subdued. India now began to shed the shackles of centuries of foreign domination. During this phase of cultural renewal, Ahilyabai's efforts were aligned closely with the vision of Ch. Shivaji Maharaj. Historian Gajanan Mehendale, describes Ch. Shivaji's three-fold mission - to rebuild destroyed temples, purify language of foreign corruptions, and Ghar-Wapasi of the converted.

The practice of reclaiming sacred spaces, initiated by Ch. Shivaji was continued by his successors like Ch. Sambhaji Raje and Nanasaheb Peshwa. The practice found its most expansive expression under Ahilyabai's reign.

Ahilyabai's era of reconstruction was a balm for a civilization that had endured a millennium of assault. As Rajat Mitra poignantly observes, the repeated destruction of temples and sacred sites inflicted a deep, multigenerational trauma on Hindu society. This wound, long unaddressed, left Hindus suffering in silence.

Ahilyabai's approach to healing this collective trauma was characterized by gentleness and quiet determination. Her temple reconstruction efforts reclaimed sacred spaces, restored lost dignity and provided a sense of justice to generations of survivors. By offering closure to the past wounds, she opened the door to a new beginning.

In the twilight of colonial rule, many visionaries carried forward Ahilyabai's torch of cultural preservation. Likes of Birla built new temples; scholars like Jagannath Shankar Shet promoted Sanskrit; Raja of Aundh promoted Yoga; Swami Vivekananda reinterpreted Vedantic philosophy; Dadasaheb Phalke retold the stories of Ramayana, Mahabharata and Purana through cinema; likes of Mahendralal Sarkar established educational institutes; Gaikwads of Baroda, Wadiyars of Mysore built dams, infrastructure, and established research institutes; Tatas laid the foundations of modern industry and leaders championed for Swarajya and Swadeshi.

These efforts were mostly from pre-independence era. Post British Raj, India faced a monumental task of cultural revival, one that echoed and amplified the efforts of Ahilyabai Holkar. The depth and breadth of British influence necessitated a comprehensive strategy for post-independence India.

Unfortunately the task of cultural revival lacked a champion in the new government. It did not receive patronage or inclusion in the development and educational policies of independent India. P. V. Kane had predicted in 1946, of impending destruction of Sanskrit learning and Indology after attaining Independence, which unfortunately came true.

Ahilyabai's cultural rejuvenation post Mughal Rule included:

1. Temple reconstruction
2. Promotion of Sanskrit language
3. Use of local language in administration
4. Promoting reading of the scriptures
5. Codifying Hindu Acharan

Despite this blueprint, independent India largely perpetuated British systems in education, judiciary, and administration. The continued dominance of English in these spheres stands in stark contrast to other former colonies like Sri Lanka, Burma, Indonesia, Malaysia, Thailand, Vietnam etc. that adopted their native languages post-independence.

The task of cultural revival Post British Rule needed efforts far beyond Ahilyabai's time, including:

1. **Temple Restoration:**
   - Temple rebuilding, and restoring.
   - Reinstating temple lands, gardens, meditation spaces, lecture halls, schools, performance venues, goshalas, akhadas, and libraries.
   - Restoring temple autonomy in management.
   - Without a deity some temples have reduced to monuments. Reinstalling deities in such temples and bringing them back to life.

2. **Language and Education:**
   - Making mathematical, scientific, and technical knowledge available in regional languages.
   - Use of local language in administrative and judicial processes.
   - Reintroducing ethics and morals from Hindu scriptures into curricula.
   - Promoting Sanskrit

3. **Indigenous Industries and Knowledge:**
   - Reviving traditional knowledge in various fields.
   - Revitalizing indigenous industries

4. **Sacred Geographies and Timeless Histories:**
   - Restoring the sanctity of ancient temples; they are not mere tourist attractions.
   - Reconnecting people with the spiritual landscape
   - Reconnecting people to their eternal roots through the ancient histories narrated in texts.

5. **Cultural Confidence:**
   - Fostering pride in Indian cultural heritage.
   - Encouraging critical engagement with tradition rather than blind imitation of Western models.

The scale of this task is immense, requiring sustained, long-term efforts from political, educational, judicial, and spiritual leaders. It calls for visionaries in the mold of Ahilyabai, who can bridge the gap between ancient wisdom and modern needs.

Challenges in this cultural revival require –

- Overcoming the colonial mindset

- Balancing rich traditions with the demands of a globalized world.

- A fundamental shift in mindset - from seeing Indian culture as something to be preserved in museums to recognizing it as a living and evolving force that can guide India's future.

This revival is not about turning back the clock, but about reclaiming the essence of Indian civilization and adapting it to meet the challenges of the 21st century. The unfinished work of cultural revival remains a crucial task.

UNIFIED, SACRED BHARAT

Unified India of Ahilyabai's vision offers a stark contrast to the later colonial perspective. Key aspects of Ahilyabai's vision include:

1. Sacred Geography:
As put forth by the Hindu scriptures, Ahilyabai viewed India as one nation - from the Himalayas to the Ocean. Where the British saw it as separate nations based on its different languages.

For Ahilyabai this land, with its rivers and mountains was a sacred place to be revered and nurtured. Unlike the British who regarded the same land as a colony / market / resource to be exploited and plundered.

2. Divine Beings:

Guided by Hindu philosophy, Ahilyabai perceived *Paramatma* in every living being. Thus she ensured that in her kingdom humans and animals alike were well-fed.

In contrast, the Indians were "a beastly people with a beastly religion" as infamously articulated by UK Prime Minister Winston Churchill. Such attitude led to the death of about 20 million Indians in the artificially created famines during British rule.

3. Unity in Diversity:

Devi patronized various sects and traditions, from Shaiva to Vaishnava and from Varakari Panth to Ramadasi Panth. Her inclusive approach strengthened Hindu unity. Ahilyabai viewed all Indians as her praja (children), transcending boundaries of region, language, caste and sect.

Ahilyabai's unite-and-empower approach contrasted sharply with the British divide-and-rule policy.

4. Cultural Pride and Preservation:

As a devout Hindu, Ahilyabai took pride in Indian culture and traditions. She held Shruti, Smruti, Itihas, and Puranas in high esteem, actively promoting their study and dissemination.

British on the other hand dismissed the texts as mythologies. This allegation, particularly amongst the English educated Hindus, replaced *shraddha* (faith) with scepticism. It distanced the people from a source of their ancient knowledge, which was akin to separating babies from their nursing mothers.

5. Economic Self-Reliance:

Ahilyabai developed local industries, particularly the textile industry in Maheshwar. She encouraged the use of indigenous products, a precursor to the later Swadeshi movement.

This stood in stark contrast to the British deindustrialization of India and later introducing the system of "Indentured Labor".

6. Empowerment of Spiritual Institutions:

Ahilyabai strengthened temples through land endowments and the establishment of associated institutions like schools and Dharmashalas. This holistic approach preserved temples as centers of learning and community development.

7. Holistic Development:

Ahilyabai's governance focused on spiritual, cultural, ecological and material well-being. Her projects, from temple reconstruction to establishing Sanskrit schools and from tree plantations to support for businesses and industries exemplify it.

The stark contrast between the exploitative approach of the colonial rule and Ahilyabai's nurturing governance can be traced to the fundamental difference in their perspectives on – Hindus, Hinduism and Hindustan. This distinction, in fact, will separate every benevolent ruler from the not so benevolent one. The criteria applies to elected governments too.

Ahilyabai saw the land as sacred, every river worthy of worship and every living being as a manifestation of

Paramatma, a view deeply influenced by the teachings of Itihas and Puranas. The reverence for the land, its culture, its Dharma, its scriptures and its people underpinned her compassionate, effective and welfare rule.

For Ahilyabai, progress came not from rejecting one's heritage, but from building upon it. Her vision presents a roadmap for cultural revival and national integration that remains relevant even today.

Her legacy challenges modern leaders to view India not just as a nation-state, but as a living, breathing civilization with a sacred geography, timeless history and a deeply spiritual heritage.

Her story is a guide for the future, offering insights into how India can move forward while remaining true to her civilizational roots. Had the tradition of writing Puranas continued to this day, she would have become the subject of one. The Puranas would have recorded her story as a lesson for the future leaders and citizens of India.

The histories of the temples rebuilt by Ahilyabai Holkar chronicle a civilization's determined efforts to survive and preserve its holy spaces. By rescuing and rebuilding hundreds of temples, she spared future generations the pain of witnessing ruins and the distress of seeing domes atop what once were grand temples.

In recent times, the reclamation and reconstruction of the Ram Janmabhoomi (RJB) temple revealed the lingering wounds of past traumas. The struggle to rebuild this temple saw immense sacrifices, with thousands of devotees losing their lives. The efforts led to significant political upheaval, including the dismissal of several democratically elected Bharatiya Janata Party (BJP) state governments by the central Indian National Congress government. The conflict was marked by widespread riots in India. The Hindus of Bangladesh and Pakistan were also not spared, where hundreds of Hindu temples were destroyed, their shops and homes were burnt down. The Central Government's inability to handle the issue with the same calm and subtlety as Ahilyabai had exacerbated the conflict.

After the BJP Govt led by PM Narendra Modi, came to power, the RJB issue was resolved through judicial processes in a civilized manner. Had the earlier governments taken cues from Ahilyabai's amicable methods, Hindus of the subcontinent would have been spared of much trauma.

Somnath temple is believed to have been built by Soma, the moon god, which was later renovated by Shri Krishna. King Dharsen of Maitrak dynasty built a grand temple here in the 7th century. The majestic temple had bells of gold, doors of sandalwood, ornate pillars and gems studded walls.

Somnath faced numerous invasions and destructions notably by Md. of Ghazni in the 11th century and by Alauddin Khilji in the 13th century. Each time, the temple was rebuilt by Hindus, symbolizing resilience and devotion. The temple was destroyed yet again by Aurangzeb in the early 18th century and a small mosque was built within its ruins. After the collapse of Mughal Empire, Junagadh Nawab assumed the control of Saurasthra.

It is said that, in a dream, location of the original Shivalinga was revealed to Ahilyabai. Acting on the vision, she had the Shivalinga retrieved from the mosque. She acquired land near the ruins of the old temple and constructed there a modest two storied temple. The original Shivalinga was installed at the lower level garbha griha. Under Ahilyabai's leadership the worship at Somnath resumed again.

Soon after independence, Sardar Vallabhbhai Patel cleared the area by moving the ruins to a museum, the mosque a few kilometers away and building the current grand Somnath temple. A new Shivalinga was installed at the hands of the then President of India, Dr. Rajendra Prasad.

Recently, PM Narendra Modi led the renovation of the temple precincts that included the construction of a grand promenade along the coast and foundation for a new Parvati temple. The Shiva Mandir built by Ahilyabai Holkar has also been renovated and expanded.

VISHWANATH, UTTAR PRADESH

Varanasi situated on banks of Assi and Varana is also called Kashi, the city of light or knowledge. It is India's religious, cultural and educational capital since time immemorial. This sacred land of Shiva is believed to give Moksha (liberation from cycle of birth and death).

Beginning from the 11th century, Shiva temple at Kashi was destroyed by Islamist invaders time and again. It was rebuilt by Hindu kings, merchants and Sadhus each time it was fallen. Aurangzeb destroyed the temple and built domes of Gyanvapi Mosque on its ruins.

The Marathas, right from Ch. Shivaji to Madhavrao Peshwa intended to reclaim Kashi, Mathura and Ayodhya, but were unable to do so in their lifetimes. In 1777, Ahilyabai acquired land near the site and constructed a small temple of Kashi Vishwanath. About a hundred years after the last demolition the worship of Vishwanath had been reinstated.

Maharaja Ranjit Singh the founder of Sikh empire gilded the Vishwanath temple spire in gold.

In 2021, under PM Narendra Modi, the temple area was expanded and a wide Kashi Vishvanath Corri-dor was constructed to connect the temple to the river Ganga.

GHIRISHNESHWAR, MAHARASHTRA

This temple at Verul (Ellora) had been attacked sever-al times. It was repaired by Maloji Raje Bhosale, the grandfather of Ch. Shivaji. Later, it was attacked by Aurangzeb. The half destroyed temple lay in ruins for years. Gautamabai Holkar started its reconstruction in 1730. It was taken to completion by her daughter-in-law Ahilyabai Holkar.

TRETA KE THAKUR, AYODHYA

Ayodhya had three main temples of Rama, the Janmasthan temple (the birthplace of Rama), the Treta-Ke-Thakur temple (place where Rama per-formed the Ashvamedha Yajna) and the Swargadwar temple (place from where Rama left the mortal world).

Of these Babur destroyed and built a mosque at the Janmasthan temple. Aurangzeb destroyed and built mosques at Treta-ke-Thakur and Swargadwar.

In 1784, the Maratha queen Ahilyabai, bought the Treta-ke-Thakur land, and rebuilt a temple there. It is said that the original murti were found from the river Sharayu and installed here.

Statues of Devi Ahilyabai Holkar have been erected across India, including in the Parliament House in New Delhi, her birthplace in Chondi, her capital city Maheshwar, at Somnath and at Varanasi, reflecting her contributions to Hindu Dharma and cultural heritage. The Indore airport is named after her, recognizing her contributions to infrastructure.

Recently the Ahmednagar district was renamed as Ahilyanagar to honour her legacy. Numerous educational institutions across India, including agricultural colleges and Solapur University, bear her name.

The Devi Ahilyabai Holkar Award, part of the Nari Shakti Puraskar, is given annually by the Ministry of Women and Child Development to organizations promoting women's welfare. Postal stamps have been issued in her honour.

Devi's exemplary life and effective governance inspired poets and writers to pen tributes to her. Among them, Khushali Ram Bhatt, Moropant and Anant Fandi wrote in her praise. Peshwa court poet Prabhakar composed a Powada (a heroic poem) in her praise. Modern poet Madhav Julian drew parallels between Ahilyabai and the great Rajarshi Janaka.

Noteworthy works include Pandit Sakharam Shastri Bhagwat's Sanskrit book "Ahalya Charitam," Kumud's Marathi composition "Ahalyabai Holkar" that was written in 1885, and Hari Moreshwar Shevde's "Ahalya Charitra" penned in 1898. Her life, character, and achievements have been extensively documented in various languages including Marathi, Hindi, English, Sanskrit, Bangla, Gujarati, Urdu, and Punjabi.

Sir John Malcolm (b.1769 - d.1833) visited Maheshwar and meticulously documented her life and reign in his two-volume work 'A Memoir of Central India, including Malwa' It was published in 1824 from London.

Joanna Baillie (b.1762 - d.1851), a Scottish poet, read Malcolm's Memoirs. Captivated by Ahilyabai's life and works, she composed 'Ahalya Baee, A Poem' its last stanza goes—

> In better days from Brahma came,
> to rule our land a noble Dame,
> kind was her heart, and bright her fame,
> and Ahalya was her honoured name!

REFERENCES

1. होळकरशाहीचा इतिहास – संपादक वा. वा. ठाकूर, होळकर स्टेट प्रेस, इंदोर १९४६

2. होळकर कुलभूषण अहिल्यादेवी डॉ. सुलोचना अशोक पाटील

3. ज्ञात-अज्ञात अहिल्याबाई - विनया खडपेकर, राजहंस

4. वेध अहिल्याबाईंचा – देविदास पोटे

5. कर्मयोगिनी – विजया जहागीरदार, चेतश्री प्रकाशन, १९९१

6. तेजस्विनी अहिल्याबाई होळकर – विजया जहागीरदार, महाराष्ट्र राज्य साहित्य आणि संस्कृती मंडळ, २००३

7. काशी संस्कृत ग्रंथमाला १८५ - श्री महर्षी शुक्राचार्य विरचित शुक्रनीति: - व्याख्याकार श्री पं ब्रह्म शंकर मिश्र:

8. Ahalya Baee – Joanna Baillie: Ahilyanjali, Tr. by N. G. Kale, Ahilyabai Holkar Smarak Samiti, 2015

9. Memoirs of Central India Sir John Malcom

10. Life & Life's work of Shri Devi Ahilyabai Holkar - V. V. Thakur, Indore

11. Subhedar Malhar Rao Holkar: Founder of the Indore State - Mukund Wamanrao Burway (1930)

12. Malwa Through The Ages By Kailash Chand Jain; Motilal Banarasidas, Delhi 1972

13. Flight Of Deities And Rebirth Of Temples: Meenakshi Jain (2019), Aryan Books International

14. Hindu Temples: What Happened To Them? Volume 1 & 2 – Sita Ram Goel, Voice of India, New Delhi

15. A For Ahilyabai – Edited by Devidas Pote; Ahilyabai Holkar Smarak Samiti, Dec 2015

16. Subhedar Malhar Rao Holkar: Founder of the Indore State - Mukund Wamanrao Burway (1930) Available at - archive.org

17. Al-Hind: Making of the Indo-Islamic World, vol. 1, Brill Academic (Leiden), Andre Wink (1991)

18. What Happens when a Hindu Temple is Destroyed - Sandeep Balakrishna; The Dharma Dispatch, Sep 2018 Available at - dharmadispatch.in

19. The Illustrated Encyclopedia Of Hinduism - James Lochtefeld Page 298

20. Epigraphia Indica Vol 8 (1905-06) Edited By E. Hultzsch, Available at - archive.org

21. The Vijayanagar Empire Chronicles Of Paes And Nuniz; Available at archive.org

22. The Great Maratha Mahadaji Scindia - N. G. Rathod (1994), Sarup & Sons. pp. 163–173

23. New History Of The Marathas Vol.2 by Sardesai, Govind Sakharam, page 338

24. Solstice at Panipat – Uday Kulkari, Mula Mutha Publishers, Pune

25. Goa Inquisition - The Terrible Tribunal For The East - Anant Kakba Priolkar

26. Parish Churches in the Early Modern World edited by Andrew Spicer

27. Lost treasures : Temples Demolished by Mughals and other Invaders - Ponnam Chetan, pages 28-29

28. The Beautiful Tree – Dharmapal, 1983, Other India Press

29. Shivaji and His Times: Route of Shivaji's flight – Jadunath Sarkar available at archive.org

30. India in the Victorian age - Dutt, Romesh (1904); London; Page 524, 525 Available at – archive.org

31. Shri Ramakrishna Paramahans: The Great Master by Swami Saradanand, Translated by Swami Jagadanand; Published by Shri Ramakrishna Math, Madras

32. Isabel Burton (2012). Arabia, Egypt, India: A Narrative of Travel. Cambridge University Press. p. 168.

33. Asia and Oceania: International Dictionary of Historic Places - Trudy Ring, Noelle Watson, Paul Schellinger 2012

34. India's Historic Battles: From Alexander the Great to Kargil By Kaushik Roy, Permanent Black (2004)

35. Romanies and the Holocaust: A reevaluation and an overview - Ian Hancock, The Historiography of the Holocaust Palgrave-Macmillan, New York 2004, pp. 383-396

36. Anant Fandi; Marathi Vishvakosh

37. Hebbale Inscription- Unremembered Miniature of Hoysala Service to Sanatana Dharma - S Balkrishnan, At dharmadispatch.in

38. Sawai Jai Singh Destroys Jizya Tax - Shatavadhani Dr. R Ganesh Available at - prekshaa.in

39. Aundhacha Raja - G. D. Madgulakar, Yuvak Bharati

40. The Rajarshi of Mysore, Jun 6, 2009, Banglore Mirror, Available at- bangaloremirror.indiatimes.com

41. Shri Narayan Bhatt: Redefining the Pilgrimage in 16th Century Braj - Sushant Bharti, indica.today

42. A Trauma that lives on in many present day Indians- Rajat Mitra Available on - rajatmitra.co.in

43. Why does The Hindu Become Silent When His Temples Are Desecrated? Rajat Mitra, Jul 04, 2019, MyIndMakers Available at myind.net

44. Coronation Ceremony of Shivaji the Great - A speech by Gajanan Mehendale, 31 May 2020

45. 'A nation stays alive when its culture stays alive' - Paul Smith, British Council, June 2017

46. Jejuri Lake - Rahul Vavare, At ahilyabaiholkar.in

47. Holakar Kalin Pushkarni – R Lande, At ahilyabaiholkar.in

48. Ready Reckoner of Aurangzeb's Industrial Scale Temple Destructions - May 2022, Available at dharmadispatch.in

49. Temple Economics – Sandeep Singh

50. Revisiting Sati - Nithin Sridhar, Nov 2017, Available on IndiaFacts

51. Madhyarekha: The ancient Indian astronomical median line - Sachin Jadhav, Available on Medium.com

52. Harkuvar Sethani Mansion- Available at heritage.ahmedabadcity-.gov.in

53. 'Natorer Rani' Bhabani, Daily Bangladesh Aug 2019, Available at - daily-bangladesh.com

54. Real Rani - Rani Rashmoni merged philanthropy and business; available at getbengal.com

55. The Impending Destruction of Sanskrit: What P.V. Kane Predicted in 1946 - Sandeep Balakrishna, Aug 2024, Dharma Dispatch, Available on- dharmadispatch.in

Deepali Patwadkar is a masterful storyteller who brings Indian culture alive for contemporary audiences. She serves as adjunct faculty member for Indian Knowledge Systems and for Epic Studies.

Her literary footprint includes – '*Rāmakathā-Mālā*', '*The Flags of Bhārata*', and '*Illustrated Dnyaneshwari: Karma Yoga*'.

She writes regularly through prestigious publications including – Maharashtra Times, Sakal and Mumbai Tarun Bharat. Her scholarly works extend to peer-reviewed journals and columns in Saptahik Vivek, Prasad and News Bharati.

Deepali's book on Ahilyabai is more than just a historical account—it is a testament to the timeless wisdom of Indian scriptures and their role in shaping visionary leadership. Through the extraordinary life of Devi Ahilyabai Holkar, the book emphasizes how adherence to dharmic principles and insights drawn from ancient Indian texts can mold administrators capable of fostering justice, culture, and prosperity.

Ahilyabai's governance was deeply rooted in the teachings of the scriptures, which guided her decisions and shaped her as an ideal ruler. From temple restoration to welfare schemes, her administrative brilliance stemmed from values and ethics taught by the scriptures. The book illustrates how such values can nurture leadership that is both compassionate and transformative.

This inspiring work is a clarion call to revisit the Indian scriptures—not as relics of the past, but as living guides to train future administrators and nation-builders. It reminds us that the cultural and moral foundations laid out in our texts remain as relevant today as they were in Ahilyabai's era.

For anyone seeking to understand the intersection of Indic wisdom and governance, this book is a must-read. It is not just a story of a remarkable queen but also a guide for nurturing a new generation of leaders grounded in the ethos of Bharat.

- Nilesh Oak
Researcher, Speaker and Author of - "When Did The Mahabharata War Happen?", "The Historic Rama" and "Bhishma Nirvana"

9 798896 322504